CB126786

MICKEY ROGERS
JOANNE TAYLORE-KNOWLES
STEVE TAYLORE-KNOWLES

SPEAK YOUR MIND

STUDENT'S BOOK
+ access to Student's App and Digital Workbook

1B

macmillan education

	Outcomes	Vocabulary	Grammar	Speaking
Unit 7 Fit for Life pp. 67–75	• Talk about parts of the body and abilities • Talk about sports and athletes • Describe skills and abilities	• Parts of the body • Ball game action words • Exercise words	• *Can/can't* (ability) • Adverbs of manner Grammar Reference pp. 151–152	• Talk about abilities • Describe a famous athlete • Role-play a job interview
	Language and Life—Decision-making: Design an Outdoor Gym for Your City			
Unit 8 Foodie? pp. 77–85	• Talk about food and tastes • Talk about types of food and ingredients • Follow and write a recipe	• Food and tastes • Food groups • Cooking	• Countable and uncountable nouns • *This/that/these/those* Grammar Reference pp. 152–153	• Talk about food preference • Discuss and recommend healthy foods • Discuss recipes
	Language and Life—Communication: Design a Restaurant Guide			
Unit 9 Seeing the World pp. 87–95	• Talk about travel • Give advice and suggestions • Talk about clothes to wear on a trip	• Travel • Tourism collocations • Clothes	• Verb + infinitive or gerund • *Should/could* for advice and possibility Grammar Reference pp. 154–155	• Plan a virtual tour • Role-play a phone conversation • Discuss a planned trip
	Language and Life—Collaboration: Create an Advertisement to Attract Tourists			
Unit 10 Life Stories pp. 97–105	• Talk about life events • Talk about your social life • Describe a personal experience	• From the reading • Social life collocations • Collocations with *get, have,* and *make*	• Simple past (affirmative statements) • Simple past (negative statements and questions) Grammar Reference pp. 155–156	• Talk about milestones • Discuss events in the past • Talk about a specific experience from the past
	Language and Life—Empathy: Give Advice Based on Your Experience for an Advice Column			
Unit 11 Planning Ahead pp. 107–115	• Talk about plans and intentions • Give and receive advice for saving money • Talk about career goals	• To-do lists • Money • Career plans collocations	• *Going to* • Direct and indirect objects Grammar Reference pp. 157–158	• Talk about predictions and plans • Role-play a conversation about saving money • Discuss career plans
	Language and Life—Self-direction: Make a Career Plan Based On Your Interests			
Unit 12 The Great Outdoors pp. 117–125	• Discuss climate and weather • Talk about natural features in geography • Describe outdoor activities	• From the reading • Natural features • Adjectives to describe natural features	• Comparative adjectives • Review of tenses Grammar Reference pp. 158–159	• Discuss weather • Talk about a natural place • Talk about outdoor activities
	Language and Life—Problem-solving: Present Ideas for Developing a Natural Area			

Confident Communicator	Pronunciation	Listening/Reading	Thinking Skills	Writing
Start Talking • Useful phrases *Start Talking* • Buy time *Keep Talking* • Use imagination	• *Can/can't*	Read a magazine article about fitness gadgets • Skill—Read for gist Listen to people describe unusual sports • Skill—Listen for the main idea Listen to descriptions of exercises • Skill—Listen for specific information	• Analyze • Deduce • Evaluate	Write an email inquiring about a job
Unit Review p. 76 **Study Skills** p. 133—Effective Group Work				
Start Talking • Useful phrases *Keep Talking* • Useful phrases *Repair It* • Check for understanding	• Emphasis with *this/that/these/those*	Read posts from an online food forum • Skill—Read for the main idea Listen to an interview with street food vendors • Skill—Listen for specific information Listen to the steps of a recipe • Skill—Listen for specific information	• Apply • Analyze • Evaluate	Write a recipe
Unit Review p. 86 **Follow A Pro** p. 134—A Food Stylist ▶ A Baker				
Keep Talking • Take time to think *Keep Talking* • Useful phrases *Start Talking* • Follow-up questions	• *to*	Read an article about virtual travel • Skill—Scan Listen to a radio show about tourism • Skill—Listen for detail Listen to people talk about packing for a trip • Skill—Listen for gist	• Analyze • Recall • Deduce	Write advice for tourists
Unit Review p. 96 **Study Skills** p. 135—Formal vs. Informal Writing				
Start Talking • Useful phrases *Keep Talking* • Show interest *Start Talking* • Useful phrases	• the ending *–ed*	Read a biography on Malala Yousafzai • Skill—Scan for information Listen to a conversation about social life • Skill—Listen for main ideas Listen to personal stories • Skill—Listen for gist	• Summarize • Evaluate • Analyze	Write an email about a personal experience
Unit Review p. 106 **Follow A Pro** p. 136—An Event Organizer ▶ A Tour Guide				
Start Talking • Useful phrases *Keep Talking* • Suggest alternatives *Repair It* • Useful phrases	• *Going to*	Read an article about to-do lists • Skill—Read for the main idea Listen to a radio show about money • Skill—Listen for specific information Listen to a podcast about dream jobs • Skill—Listen for gist	• Apply • Calculate • Analyze	Write a journal entry about career plans
Unit Review p. 116 **Study Skills** p. 137—Personal Development				
Keep Talking • Useful phrases *Keep Talking* • Show interest *Keep Talking* • Useful phrases	• /ju/	Read a brochure about the Galapagos Islands • Skill—Scan for specific information Listen to a radio interview about waterfalls • Skill—Listen for specific information Listen to a conversation about visiting natural places in Mexico • Skill—Listen for detail	• Understand • Induce • Recall	Write a guidebook entry about a natural feature
Unit Review p. 126 **Follow A Pro** p. 138—A Forest Ranger ▶ A Botanist				

Grammar Quiz: What Do You Already Know?

A Choose the correct option.

1 I'm am not / I'm not / I isn't Brazilian.
2 Am / Is / Are your teacher from Peru?
3 It's / It / It not nice to meet you.
4 Where be / is / are they from?
5 What is / are / does your last name?
6 We am / is / are not Spanish students.

B Complete the paragraph with the simple present form of the verbs in parentheses.

Many students **1** ______________ (not know) what they want to do after they finish college. But I do. I **2** ______________ (want) to be a flight attendant. Flight attendants **3** ______________ (travel) the world, and I **4** ______________ (love) to travel! My friend Beth **5** ______________ (work) as a flight attendant now. She **6** ______________ (not make) a lot of money, but she's happy.

C Complete the sentences with the present progressive form of the verbs in the box.

cook   not do   not listen   rain   wear   work

1 It ______________ outside. Don't forget to take your umbrella.
2 The teacher is angry because the students ______________.
3 Harry has a great job. He ______________ at the office in Spain right now.
4 Sorry, I can't talk right now. I ______________ dinner.
5 Calvin ______________ the laundry now because he doesn't have any soap.
6 Dan ______________ shorts and a T-shirt because it's very hot today.

D Unscramble and write sentences.

1 listen / we / to / sometimes / music / .
____
2 I / where / vegetables / buy / can / ?
____
3 never / is / our / teacher / late / .
____
4 hair / long / Sally / has / brown / .
____
5 there / many / eggs / how / are / ?
____
6 cook / does / Adam / how / often / ?
____

E Find one error in each sentence. Write the correct sentence.

1 My fathers' name is Antonio.
____
2 Please take a umbrella with you.
____
3 Why do you have three cell phone?
____
4 Don't to forget to come to my party.
____
5 Jeff take the train to work.
____
6 We have any tomatoes.
____

Go to the Grammar Review on pages 140–141.

UNIT 7

Fit for Life

WHAT DO YOU ALREADY KNOW?

1 **Think of words you know about popular sports. Write a list of words for individual sports and team sports.**

2 **IN PAIRS** **Share and compare your information. Add more words to your lists.**

Individual sports

Team sports

DISCUSS & SHARE

VIDEO

3 **IN GROUPS** **Watch the video and answer the question.**

SYM Do you prefer individual or team sports?

In this unit, you will ...

- talk about the body, abilities, sports, and exercise.
- use thinking skills: analyze, decide, and evaluate.
- read about fitness gadgets.
- use strategies to start and keep talking by buying time and using your imagination.
- use decision-making skills to design an outdoor gym for your city.
- learn tips for effective group work.

Fitness Gadgets

VOCABULARY

A IN PAIRS Look at the picture. Use words in the box to label the parts of the body.

arm back foot head knee leg shoulder neck

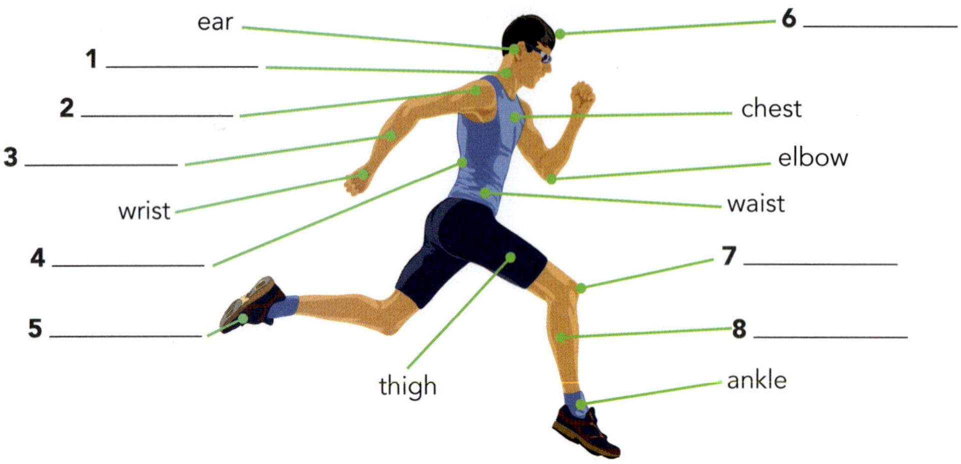

MAKE IT YOURS

Label any other parts of the body you know. Share your ideas in groups.

READING

A Match the words in the box to the pictures (1–4).

ankle sensor fitness tracker sports camera underwater headphones

____

____

____

____

B 7.01 **READING SKILL—Read for gist** Read the magazine article. Then complete with the gadget that matches the review.

New GADGET Reviews

Are you looking for a new fitness gadget? Four athletes give their opinion about these gadgets.

1 ___________ Daniella, Boston. This is great. You can wear it on your **arm** or your **ankle**. It records your steps, your calories, and your sleep. You can use it when you ride a bike, run, walk, play volleyball, do judo, and every kind of sport. $76 ★★★★½

2 ___________ Miguel, Puebla. I love swimming and listening to music at the same time. I can swim really fast when I listen to music. These go around your **neck** and fit in your **ears**. They're very comfortable. $200 ★★★½

3 ___________ Felix, Sagres. It can take videos when I'm surfing. But when I'm on my surfboard, I can't hold it in my **hand**. I put it on my surfboard instead. You can also wear it on your **head** or on your **shoulder**. It takes pictures, too. $152 ★★★★

4 ___________ Clare, Santa Fe. You wear it on your **foot** and it checks that you're running correctly. Can you wash it? No, you can't wash it, even when it's dirty. It's expensive, in my opinion, but it's useful for professional runners. $120 ★★½

C THINKING SKILL—Analyze Take a class survey. What gadgets do your classmates think are useful? Do you agree?

GRAMMAR *can/can't* (ability)

A **Read the magazine article in READING B again. Underline the sentences with *can* and *can't*.**

B **Choose the correct option to complete the rules.**

1 Use *can/can't* to talk about ...	**a** habits.	**b** abilities.
2 After *can/can't*, use a ...	**a** verb.	**b** noun.
3 The contraction of *cannot* is ...	**a** cant.	**b** can't.

For more practice, go to page 151.

C **Rewrite the sentences correctly.**

1. I can to play cricket. ______
2. She cans dance. ______
3. Can not you swim? ______
4. Yes, I can't. ______
5. He no can't play tennis. ______

D **IN PAIRS Ask and answer questions about the sports you can and can't do.**

PRONUNCIATION *can/can't*

A **7.02 Listen. Choose the words you hear.**

1. Can / Can't you swim?
2. I can / can't.
3. Can / Can't you come to a new water polo class with me?
4. Sorry, I can / can't. I play tennis then.

B **IN PAIRS Practice saying the conversation. Notice the /t/ sound in *can't*.**

SPEAKING

A **Check (✓) the things you can or can't do. Complete with your own ideas.**

	Can	Can't
1 play soccer	☐	☐
2 sing	☐	☐
3 cook Italian food	☐	☐
4 ______	☐	☐
5 ______	☐	☐

B **IN GROUPS Ask and answer questions about your abilities. Discuss information about what you like or dislike. Use the Confident Communicator box to help you.**

A: Can you surf? *B: Yes, I can, and I really enjoy it.*

CONFIDENT COMMUNICATOR
START TALKING

To ask about abilities and likes, use these phrases:
Can you ...?
Yes, I can ..., and I really enjoy it.
Yes, I can ..., but I don't really like it.
No, I can't ..., but I can ... Can you ...?

Unusual Ball Games

VOCABULARY ball game action words

A IN PAIRS Match the verbs from the box to the pictures (1–8).

bounce	catch	hit	hold
kick	pass	throw	touch

1

2

3

4

5

6

7

8

B Choose the correct option.

1. Basketball players can **bounce** / **kick** the ball during the game.
2. In soccer, the players use their feet to **pass** / **hold** the ball.
3. Lacrosse players **hold** / **catch** the ball in a net.
4. Football players **throw** / **bounce** the ball between them.
5. You **kick** / **hit** the ball with a bat in baseball.
6. Tennis players usually **hold** / **kick** the ball in their left hand when they serve.

C IN PAIRS Think about popular ball games in your country. Talk about what the players can and can't do with the ball.

In basketball, players can bounce the ball. They can't kick the ball.

LISTENING

A Look at the pictures and think about the questions.

1. What do you know about these sports?
2. Do they look like other sports you know?

Bossaball

360ball

footgolf

B 7.03 LISTENING SKILL—Listen for the main idea **Listen and write the name of the ball games from A.**

1 David: ______________.   **2** Claudia: ______________.   **3** Marco: ______________.

C IN PAIRS THINKING SKILL—Deduce **Think about the three sports you learned about and discuss the question.**

Which game do you think people your age want to play?

MAKE IT REAL

When people talk about the sports they do regularly, they often leave out the verb *go*.
I hike. = *I go hiking.*
I swim. = *I go swimming.*

GRAMMAR adverbs of manner

A Read the examples. Then complete the rules.

I can throw the ball hard.
You have to play fast.
My friend plays it well.
You have to kick the ball gently.
I can kick it easily.

1. Use adverbs of manner to describe **an action** / **a thing**.
2. Adverbs of manner go **before** / **after** the main verb.
3. To form an adverb of manner, add ______________ to the adjective.
4. When a word ends in *–y*, add ______________.
5. Some irregular adverbs are the same word as the adjective: *fast–fast, hard–*______________.
6. One irregular adverb looks completely different from the adjective: *good–*______________.

For more practice, go to page 151.

B Choose the correct form of the adverb or adjective.

1. Please drive **careful** / **carefully**.
2. Fernando is a **slow** / **slowly** swimmer.
3. Todd is a fast runner. He runs **good** / **well**.
4. This is a library. Please speak **quiet** / **quietly**.
5. Patti speaks **angry** / **angrily** to me sometimes.

C IN PAIRS **Write activities from the unit in your notebook. Add adverbs to the things you can and can't do. Then ask and answer questions.**

A: I can't cook Italian food well. Can you?   *B: No, I can't, but I can run fast.*

SPEAKING

A IN PAIRS **Make a list of famous athletes that you know and the sports that they play.**

B IN PAIRS **Play a game. Describe a famous athlete in one sentence. Your partner tries to guess who it is. Use the Confident Communicator box to help you.**

CONFIDENT COMMUNICATOR
START TALKING

Sometimes at the beginning of a conversation, you need time to organize your ideas. You can "buy time" by using these phrases:
Give me a minute to think about this …
Let me think about this for a second …

Exercising

VOCABULARY exercise words

A Match the words from the box to the exercises (1–8).

bend lift pull push stand stretch turn twist

1 
____

2 
____

3 
____

4 
____

5 
____

6 
____

7 
____

8 
____

B 7.04 Listen and complete the text.

One of the exercises that I do at the gym is very hard. It's called *the deadlift with an overhead press*. You **1** ______________ with your feet on the floor. Then, you **2** ______________ the weight (I use a 10 kilogram) up to your chest. You **3** ______________ it there for about five seconds. Then, you **4** ______________ your knees and **5** ______________ the weight up above your head. It's not easy to **6** ______________ your arms so they're straight. I can usually only hold it above my head for about 10 seconds. I'm amazed how weightlifters do this all the time!

LISTENING

A As a class, answer the question.

1 What do you think the word *deskercise* means?

B 7.05 LISTENING SKILL—Listen for specific information Listen and choose the word you hear for each exercise.

1 Exercise 1: shoulder / back
2 Exercise 2: legs / arms
3 Exercise 3: head / hand
4 Exercise 4: back / neck
5 Exercise 5: knee / foot

C 7.05 Listen again and do the exercises. How do they make you feel?

D THINKING SKILL—Evaluate Take a class survey. What parts of the body do you need to stretch when you work at a desk all day?

MAKE IT REAL

To "hit the gym" is a phrase people use when they decide to go to the gym regularly.
I need to get some exercise. I'm going to hit the gym.

WRITING

A Read the job ad. Which job are you interested in?

> **Are you free to work on weekends and holidays?**
>
> We are looking for people who can speak English to work at Our International Spa. We offer good pay, plus the use of our gym.
>
> The jobs available are:
>
> - teaching an adult volleyball class
> - working in the café
> - teaching swimming
> - working in the beauty salon
> - working at our reception desk
>
> Please email *k.smith@ourspa.co* by Friday, June 21. Be sure to send a list of your abilities.

B Make a list of your abilities in your notebook. Then decide which jobs in the ad are right for you.

C Complete the email.

New Message

From: ____________

To: k.smith@ourspa.co Cc Bcc

Subject: Employment at Our International Spa

Dear Sir/Madam,

I'm writing about a job at Our International Spa. I am ____________ years old and I live in ____________.

I'm interested in the job of ____________.

I think I am a good person for this job because ____

____.

I look forward to hearing from you.

Regards,

____________.

Send

SPEAKING

A IN PAIRS **Role-play a job interview. Use the Confident Communicator box to help you.**

Student A: You are K. Smith, the spa owner. Ask questions about why Student B wants the job.
Student B: Answer Student A's questions. Say why you are good for the job.

A: What job are you interested in? *B: I'm interested in … because …*

CONFIDENT COMMUNICATOR
KEEP TALKING

In speaking exercises in class, you don't need to say something that is true about yourself. The important thing is to say something. When you can't think of anything true to say, use your imagination.

Language and Life

Decision-making – Outdoor Gyms

A **Look at the pictures and discuss the question as a class.**

1 Where do you like to exercise?

B 7.06 **Read the article. Then answer the questions below.**

Outdoor Gyms Around the World

Many cities around the world have outdoor gyms. You see them on the beaches of Rio de Janeiro and in the parks in Shanghai or Spain. Here are some different outdoor gyms from around the world.

▶ There is a famous outdoor gym called Muscle Beach in California, USA. Bodybuilders, weightlifters, athletes, and gymnasts train here. It's now a popular tourist attraction and you can buy a ticket to go see the place!

▶ China has many outdoor gyms. This is the outdoor gym in the People's Park in Haikou. About 40% of China's 1.4 billion people use outdoor gyms regularly, according to Top.me. There are about 600,000 outdoor gyms in the country. They are all free!

▶ A new outdoor gym in Sunnymead Park in Oxford, England, has some interesting technology. When people exercise on the machines, they create electricity. The electricity creates power for streetlights, smartphones, or tablets. Amazing!

Read more

1 Which gym can you pay money to visit?
2 How many outdoor gyms are there in China?
3 Where can you exercise to help the environment?

C **IN PAIRS** **Look at the pictures and answer the question.**

1 What parts of the body do you think the pieces of equipment are good for?

I think this equipment is good for the arms and the shoulders.

1

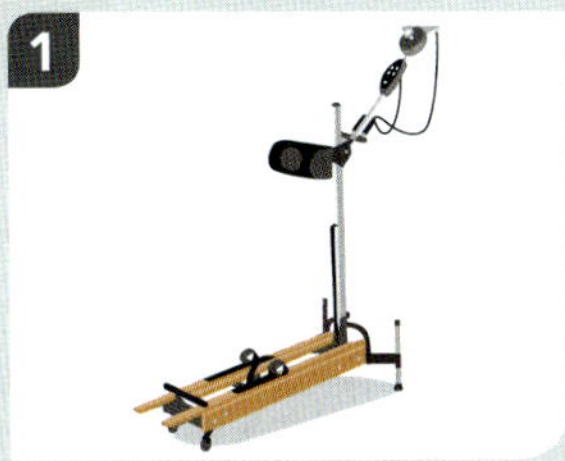

skier, $1,100

2

walker, $1,500

3

arm and leg bike, $900

4

waist twist, $1,080

5

two-person leg push, $1,110

6

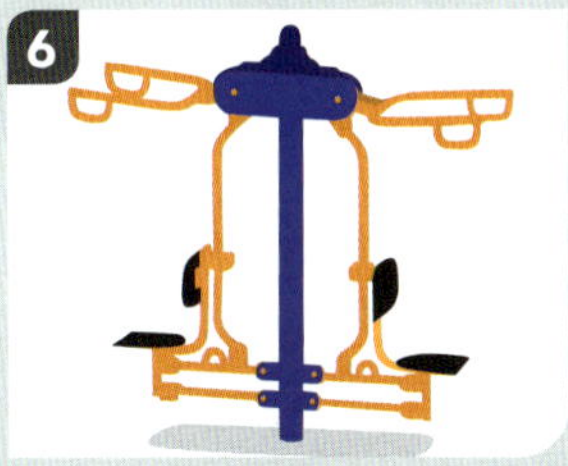

two-person pull-down, $2,300

7

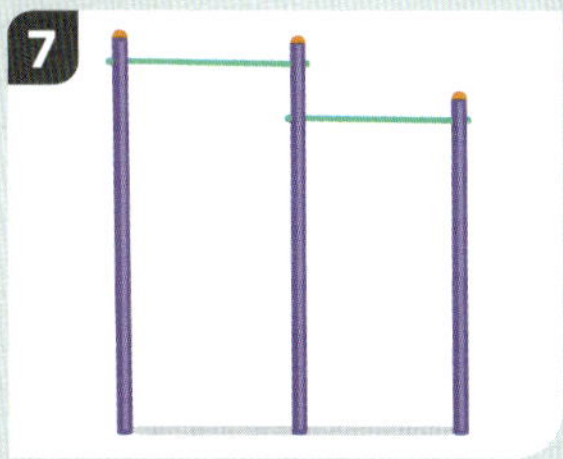

two-person pull-up, $2,300

D **Read the email and answer the question.**

1 What does the Director of Public Health want help with?

New Message

From: publichealth@gov.gov

To: citycouncil@gov.gov Cc Bcc

Subject: I need your ideas

Dear City Council Members,

We are looking at ways to help people be healthy in our city. We can have outdoor gyms in parks around the city. There is a budget of $8,000 for new gym equipment for one local park. People want equipment that is:

- for people of all ages
- easy to use
- good for different parts of the body

I look forward to hearing your ideas. Let me know what equipment is good for our park. Let's work together to create a great outdoor gym.

Regards,
The Director of Public Health

Send

E **IN GROUPS** **Imagine your group works for the city council. Look at the equipment in C. Work together to decide what to buy.**

A: I think we can get the … It's good for the …

B: I don't think we can get the … because it's expensive.
How about we get the … instead?

MAKE IT DIGITAL

Go online and find your nearest outdoor gym. What equipment does it have?

F **Share your choices with the Director of Public Health. Explain why you like this equipment.**

VOCABULARY review

SCORE: / 10

A Choose the correct option.

Almost New

Almost new fitness **1 pass / tracker**. Wear it on one **2 back / arm** while you **3 do / go** gymnastics, play **4 tennis / biking**, or any other sport. $55.

Used

Used exercise DVD. Do your daily **5 workout / kick** with trainer Danny Lee. Do **6 push-ups / baseball**, sit-ups, and other exercises to **7 get / cut** in shape fast. $10.

Almost New

Sports **8 fitness / camera**. Takes great pictures. I use it for water sports like **9 running / surfing** and swimming. Hold it in your **10 hand / shoulder** or wear it on your head. $150.

GRAMMAR review

SCORE: / 10

A Match the sentence beginning (1–5) to the sentence end (a–e). Write the letter.

1 She can't ____
2 Can you explain ____
3 Where can I ____
4 I can play ____
5 He can play soccer, ____

a volleyball and tennis.
b sing or dance.
c but he can't play rugby.
d the rules of cricket?
e buy tickets to the game?

B Complete the sentences with the adverb form of the adjectives in parentheses.

1 Baseball players need to run ________ (fast) to first base after they hit the ball.
2 Good basketball players can score 20 to 30 points in a game ________ (easy).
3 It's important for a rugby player to pass the ball ________ (careful) to another player.
4 Volleyball players near the net often hit the ball ________ (hard).
5 Soccer teams need to play ________ (good) together to win.

16–20 correct: You can talk about parts of the body and exercise words. You can use *can/can't* and adverbs of manner.
0–15 correct: Look again at the Vocabulary and Grammar sections in the unit.

TOTAL SCORE: / 20

WHAT DO YOU KNOW NOW? Look back at page 67 and add the words you know now to the boxes.

STUDY SKILLS EFFECTIVE GROUP WORK

Take the quiz on effective group work. Go to **Study Skills** on page 133 to find the answers. Then learn more about effective group work.

1 What kind of team performs best?
a a mixed-age team **b** a young-people-only team **c** a men-only team

2 You're in a meeting. Someone makes a suggestion you don't agree with. What do you say?
a "Really? Ha, ha!" **b** "That's interesting. Why do you think that?" **c** "You're wrong."

3 You're working in a group when you make a mistake. What do you say?
a "I'm sorry, my mistake." **b** "Excuse me?" **c** nothing

4 People who work alone get better results than small teams.
a true **b** false

UNIT 8

Foodie?

WHAT DO YOU ALREADY KNOW?

1 Think of words for foods that are healthy and unhealthy. Write the words.

2 IN PAIRS Share and compare your information. Add more words to your lists.

Healthy

Unhealthy

DISCUSS & SHARE

VIDEO

3 IN GROUPS Watch the video and answer the question.

SYM Do you "eat to live" or "live to eat"?

In this unit, you will ...

- talk about food, tastes, ingredients, and recipes.
- use thinking skills: apply, analyze, and evaluate.
- read about international foods.
- use strategies to repair talking by checking for understanding.
- use communication skills to design a restaurant guide.
- follow a baker to learn about this job and the skills needed for this industry.

Are You a "Gastronaut"?

READING

A IN GROUPS Look at the pictures. Do you know these foods? Do you want to try them? Discuss.

hagelslag (the Netherlands)

bunny chow (South Africa)

empanadas (Venezuela)

cendol (Malaysia)

tom yum soup (Thailand)

B 8.01 READING SKILL—Read for the main idea Read the posts from a world food forum and answer the questions.

Wendy, Canada, 5:34 says …
Hi, food fans! Do you know the word *gastronaut*? It's a person who travels and tries different foods. That's me! I love something **delicious** called *hagelslag*. It's from the Netherlands. It has small, sweet pieces of chocolate you put on bread for breakfast. My boyfriend thinks it's **disgusting**! Do you like foods from different countries? What kind? How many new dishes do you try each week?

Soraya, Bali, 9:45 says …
I'm a gastronaut, too! I love to try different foods from all over the world. My favorite food is *tom yum soup*, from Thailand. It's a spicy soup with shrimp and vegetables. I often have it for lunch. It's a very **healthy** meal! I add chilies to mine to make it extra spicy.

Peter, South Africa, 9:54 says …
Hi, Wendy! Do you know about *bunny chow*? It comes from South Africa. It's a loaf of bread, but you take the middle of the bread out and put **spicy** beef or chicken inside. How much meat do you need? It depends on how big the loaf is! We usually eat it for lunch or dinner.

Marlena, Venezuela, 11:32 says …
My favorite food is *empanadas*. They are delicious. You can make them with corn flour, water, and salt. You can put cheese, meat, chicken—anything you like—inside. Then, you fry them. Some people eat them as a **snack**. My mom thinks they are **unhealthy** because you fry them.

Ben, Scotland, 12:54 says …
I think I'm a gastronaut, too. Do you know a dessert called *cendol* from Malaysia? It's really unusual. It's green rice noodles, coconut milk, and sugar. You can also add fruit. It's very **sweet**. It looks like green spaghetti!

1 What kind of flour do you use for empanadas? ______
2 What food is from Thailand? ______
3 Is bunny chow a snack? ______
4 What is cendol? ______
5 Are you a gastronaut? Why or why not? ______

C IN PAIRS THINKING SKILL—Apply Think about a popular food in your country. What is it? When do you eat it? What is in it? Do you like it? Tell your partner.

VOCABULARY

A Find and circle all the food items in READING B.

B Match the underlined words in READING B to the definitions (1–7).

1 has the hot taste of chilies (adjective) ______
2 tastes very, very bad (adjective) ______
3 good for your body (adjective) ______
4 has the taste of sugar (adjective) ______
5 a small amount of food you eat between meals (noun) ______
6 not good for your body (adjective) ______
7 has a very good taste (adjective) ______

MAKE IT YOURS

Think about a food and a drink that you like. Use a dictionary to add the words to the vocabulary list for this lesson.

GRAMMAR countable and uncountable nouns

A Complete the examples with the foods from READING B. Then complete the rules.

Countable nouns

Singular: *a vegetable*, ______, ______, ______

Plural: *vegetables*, ______, ______

Uncountable nouns

chocolate, *bread*, ______, ______, ______, ______, ______

Questions

How many ______? *How much* ______?

1 Countable nouns are people or things you **can** / **can't** count. Use numbers and the article *a*/*an* with countable nouns.
2 Countable nouns can be **singular** / **plural** / **both singular and plural**.
3 Uncountable nouns are not **singular** / **plural**.
4 We use *How many …?* with **countable** / **uncountable** nouns.
5 We use *How much …?* with **countable** / **uncountable** nouns.

For more practice, go to page 152.

B Complete with the singular or plural form of the noun.

1 How much ______ (milk) do you want in your coffee?
2 I like ______ (banana) and ______ (grape), but I don't like ______ (orange).
3 Can I have ______ (cheese) on my pizza, please?
4 How many ______ (egg) do you want for breakfast?
5 I don't eat ______ (fish) or meat. I'm a vegetarian.

SPEAKING

A Make a list of foods you know from different countries in your notebook.

B IN PAIRS Ask and answer questions about the foods you like. Use the Confident Communicator box to help you.

C Take a class survey to see how many gastronauts are in your class. Discuss.

CONFIDENT COMMUNICATOR
START TALKING

There are different ways to ask about preferences.
Do you like Thai food? Yes, I do. / No, I don't.
Which do you prefer, chicken or fish?
I prefer chicken (to fish).
Do you prefer pasta or rice? I prefer pasta.

LESSON 2 A Balanced Diet

VOCABULARY food groups

A Look at the food group diagram. Complete the diagram with words from the box.

apples	bananas	beans	bread	butter	cereal	cheese	chocolate	corn	eggs
fish	ice cream	milk	oil	pasta	potatoes	rice	soda	chicken	yogurt

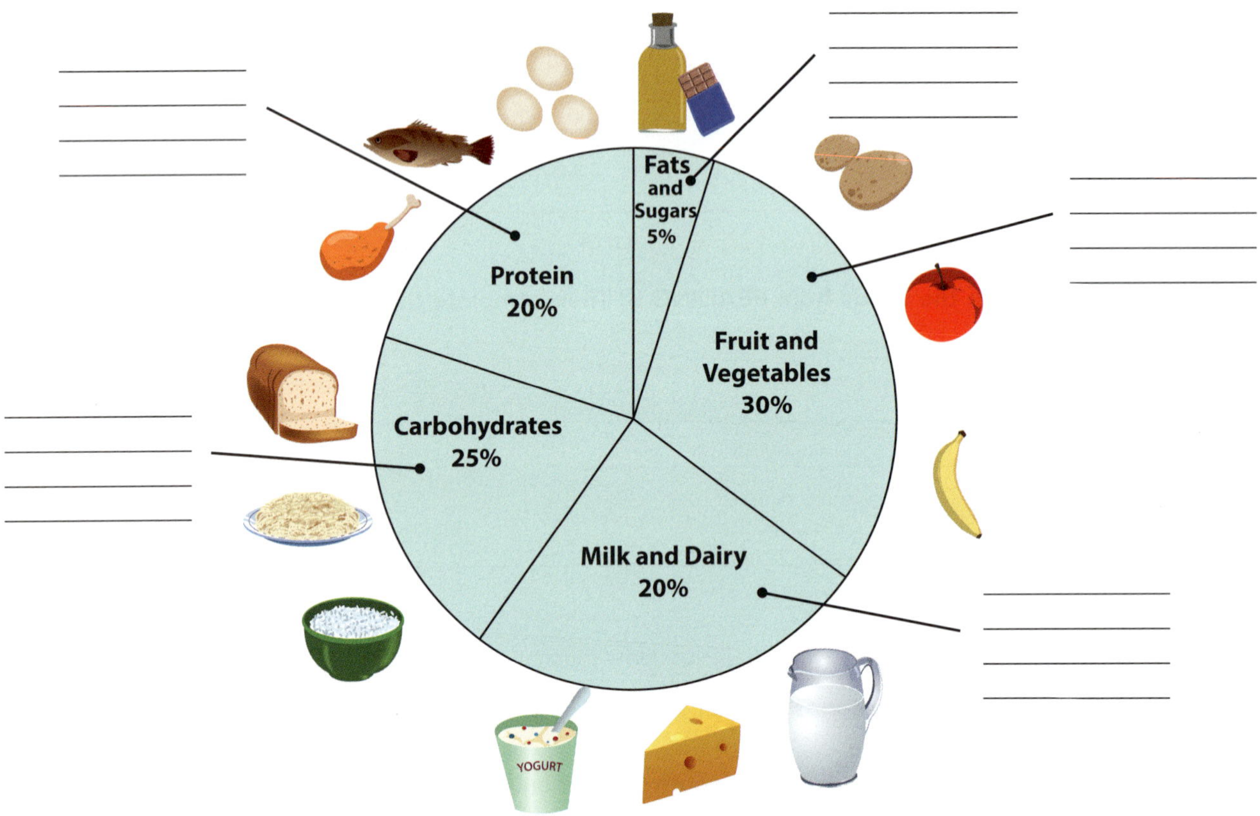

B IN PAIRS Discuss how much of each food group you eat.

I usually eat two kinds of protein a day, but I don't eat a lot of fruit and vegetables.

LISTENING

A Discuss the questions.

1 Do you like going to food markets?
2 What foods do you eat there?

B 8.02 Listen to Conversations 1 and 2 and choose *True* or *False*.

1 The interviewer thinks falafel is spicy. True / False
2 The woman says that her falafel is unhealthy. True / False
3 The bibimbap has carbohydrates, vegetables, and protein. True / False
4 The man's bibimbap is vegan. True / False

C 8.02 LISTENING SKILL—Listen for specific information Listen again and write the words you hear.

1 Food markets like this sell cheap food, but is it ______________?
2 This falafel is healthy because we grill it. Fried falafel has more ______________ and calories.
3 It looks like a/an ______________ meal!
4 So, the food at this market is ______________, and some of it is healthy, too.

D THINKING SKILL—Analyze Look up the words *vegan* and *vegetarian*. Do you think you can be vegan or vegetarian? Why or why not?

GRAMMAR *this/that/these/those*

A Read the conversation. Then complete the rules with *this/that* or *these/those*.

Shelly: Hi. Can I get a pound of apples, please?
Jon: Sure. Do you want those green ones?
Shelly: No, these apples, please. The red ones.
Jon: OK. Anything else?
Shelly: How big is that watermelon?
Jon: That one is small. It's 10 pounds.
Shelly: And this watermelon here?
Jon: This one is 15 pounds.
Shelly: OK, this one, please. Thanks.

1. Use ____________ and ____________ with singular nouns.
2. Use ____________ and ____________ with plural nouns.
3. Use ____________ and ____________ to talk about things near us.
4. Use ____________ and ____________ to talk about things not near us.

For more practice, go to page 153.

B Look at the pictures. Complete with *this, that, these,* or *those*.

1 

2 

3 

4 

1. Can we sit at ____________ table, please?
2. Can I have ____________ apples, please?
3. How much is ____________?
4. I like ____________. They're delicious.

PRONUNCIATION emphasis with *this/that/these/those*

A 8.03 Listen to the conversations. Underline the words the speakers stress.

Conversation 1
A: Is this my salad?
B: No, that's your salad.

Conversation 2
A: Are these your apples?
B: No, those are my apples.

Conversation 3
A: Do you want that snack?
B: No, I want this one.

B 8.03 Listen again and practice stressing the correct words.

SPEAKING

A IN PAIRS Discuss the difference between healthy and unhealthy foods. Make a note of the healthy and unhealthy foods you eat every day.

B IN GROUPS Make a meal plan. Discuss and recommend healthy foods that your group can eat for every meal of the day. Use the Confident Communicator box to help you.

A: Hmm. How about donuts for breakfast?
B: Well, they're very sweet.
A: How about cereal with fruit instead?
B: Yes, that's healthy.

CONFIDENT COMMUNICATOR
KEEP TALKING

It's a good idea to recommend an alternative when you give advice. Use *instead* (in place of).
How about + noun + *instead*?
e.g., *How about a sandwich instead?*

LESSON 3 Cooking

VOCABULARY cooking

A Match the words from the box to the pictures (1–10).

baking dish   bowl   measuring cup   fork   knife   spoon   add   bake   mix   slice

1

_____

2

_____

3

_____

4

_____

5

_____

6

_____

7

_____

8

_____

9

_____

10

_____

B Read the recipe for ice cream banana bread. Match the instructions (1–7) to the pictures (a–g). Write the letter.

Ice Cream Banana Bread

EASY, DELICIOUS, AND ONLY FIVE INGREDIENTS!

a

b

c

d

e

f

g

Oil
3 bananas
1 cup of flour
¼ cup of sugar
2 cups of chocolate ice cream

Oven: 175 degrees Celsius
Cooking time: 1 hour

1 Pour the mixture into the baking dish. _____
2 Put oil on the baking dish. _____
3 Bake for one hour. _____
4 Slice the bananas. _____
5 Add the flour and sugar. _____
6 Mix again with a spoon. _____
7 Put the bananas and ice cream together in a bowl and mix with a fork. _____

C **IN PAIRS** Give instructions on making ice cream banana bread.

LISTENING

A Do you cook? What do you make? Discuss as a class.

B 8.04 LISTENING SKILL—Listen for specific information Listen and complete the ingredient list.

Rainbow Pizza (a snack for 4–6 people)

Ingredients

- 2 ______________ of flour
- oil
- 1 cup of water
- 1 orange ______________
- 1 cup of ______________
- 2 cups of ______________ cheese
- 1 cup of red tomatoes
- 1 green pepper
- _____ purple onion
- salt and pepper

C 8.05 Listen and complete the instructions.

1 Put the flour in a/an ______________. Add salt and pepper. Then add the water and oil.
2 ______________ with a spoon or fork. Then use your hands to make a ball. Roll the ball into a circle.
3 Put the pizza dough on a ______________.
4 ______________ all the vegetables into small pieces. Don't mix them together.
5 Put the ______________ on the pizza dough first.
6 Make a row of ______________, then orange peppers, then corn.
7 ______________, add green peppers. Then add purple onions.
8 ______________ at 200°C for 20 minutes. Then slice.

MAKE IT REAL

I'm starving! = *I am very hungry.*
I'm stuffed! = *I can't eat more food.*

D THINKING SKILL—Evaluate Think about the questions.

1 Do you think it's important how food looks?
2 Does food that looks good usually taste good?

WRITING

A Think about food you like from your country. Choose one dish that you know how to make.

B List the ingredients in your notebook.

C Read the recipe from LISTENING C and underline the imperatives.

D Write your recipe in your notebook using imperatives.

SPEAKING

A IN PAIRS Play a game. Student A: Read the recipe slowly. Don't say the name of the dish. Student B: Guess the dish. Then change roles. Use the Confident Communicator box to help you.

CONFIDENT COMMUNICATOR
REPAIR IT

Sometimes you need to ask someone to say something again to check your understanding. There are polite ways to say this:
Can you say that again, please?
Can you repeat that?
Can you say that more slowly, please?

Language and Life

Communication – A Restaurant Guide

A 🔊 **8.06 Read the reviews from a local restaurant guide. Do you want to try the restaurants? Why?**

Many people like to eat out in a neighborhood called Paradissos. There are a lot of bars and restaurants, and food from around the world, like Thai, Japanese, Greek, French—you name it! Some of the restaurants are great for snacks, but there are some expensive restaurants, too. It's hard to know what's good and what's not, so here is our guide to the places we like in Paradissos …

Matilda's: vegetarian restaurant. Great for lunch. Healthy food.
We like: the mushroom burger and the delicious avocado salad
We don't like: the carrot cake, there are only five tables
$20 for lunch
★ ★ ★

Yu Garden: Chinese restaurant. Open evenings only.
We like: the chicken noodles and egg fried rice
We don't like: the noise, the open kitchen
$30 for 3 dishes
★ ★ ★ ★

Fred's Fish: fish and seafood restaurant. Lunch and dinner. Outdoor tables in the summer.
We like: spicy shrimp spaghetti with tomatoes
We don't like: the vegetable dishes, small portions
$40–$60
★ ★ ★ ½

Encore: French café and restaurant. Breakfast, lunch, and dinner.
We like: the steak and fries—so tasty!
We don't like: nothing—we love everything here!
$25 in the café, $70 in the restaurant
★ ★ ★ ★ ★

B Read the reviews again and complete.

Which restaurant …

1 is expensive? ____________________
2 is not open in the daytime? ____________________
3 is a good place for people who don't eat meat or fish? ____________________
4 is a good place to eat outside? ____________________

C Read the article and make notes about a restaurant you know.

Write Restaurant Reviews

Do you like eating out? Do you have a favorite restaurant? We are making an exciting new food guide for the restaurants in your area. We are looking for people like you to write the restaurant reviews. We pay $100 for every review we use.

- What's the name of the restaurant?
- What type of food does it have? (for example, French / Spanish / Chinese / breakfast / snacks / etc.)
- What do you like / not like about the restaurant?
- How much is a meal for two people?
- How many stars (out of 5) do you give it?

1 Restaurant name: __________
2 Type of food: __________
3 What you like: __________
4 What you don't like: __________
5 How much is a meal for two people?: __________
6 How many stars (out of 5)?: __________

D **IN PAIRS** Discuss your ideas.

E **IN GROUPS** Choose one restaurant using the group's notes. Write a review.

F Take a class survey. Choose a restaurant to recommend to a visitor to your area.

MAKE IT DIGITAL

Go online to look for a new dish for the restaurant to serve. Include pictures, prices, and some information about the dish to make people want to try it!

VOCABULARY review

SCORE: / 10

A Choose the word that does NOT belong.

1 Proteins: steak / corn / beans
2 Fats/Sugars: oil / butter / eggs
3 Fruits/Vegetables: grapes / rice / carrots
4 Carbohydrates: beef / bread / cereal
5 Milk/Dairy: yogurt / raisins / cheese
6 Meals: dinner / snack / breakfast
7 Cooking utensils: spoon / knife / add
8 Cooking verbs: delicious / bake / mix
9 Words to describe food: sweet / tall / disgusting
10 Healthy foods: salad / apples / donut

GRAMMAR review

SCORE: / 10

A Find and correct one error in each sentence.

1 For this recipe, you need two banana and four eggs. ____________________
2 Use a fork to mash the bananas in bowl with the eggs. ____________________
3 Pour into a pan with oils and cook on both sides. ____________________
4 Cook on both sides and top with fruit or a chocolate. ____________________
5 How much servings it makes is up to you! ____________________

B Choose the correct option.

1 Excuse me, but is **that** / **these** / **those** a vegetarian dish?
2 **These** / **This** / **Those** soup tastes delicious. Try it!
3 Waiter! **These** / **Those** / **This** vegetables don't taste good.
4 How much are **these** / **those** / **that** carrots over there?
5 Can you help me put **this** / **that** / **these** watermelon in my bag?

16–20 correct: You can talk about food and food groups. You can use countable/uncountable nouns and *this/that/these/those*.
0–15 correct: Look again at the Vocabulary and Grammar sections in the unit.

TOTAL SCORE: / 20

WHAT DO YOU KNOW NOW? Look back at page 77 and add the words you know now to the boxes.

FOLLOW A PRO — FOOD INDUSTRY

Take the quiz about food stylists. Go to **Follow A Pro** on page 134 to find the answers. Then learn more about the food industry.

1 When food stylists take pictures of breakfast cereal, what do they use instead of milk?
a white glue **b** white toothpaste **c** cream

2 Food stylists use hand soap for the top of a cappuccino.
a true **b** false

3 What do food stylists do before they photograph a roast chicken?
a put newspaper inside it **b** paint it yellow **c** cover it with nail polish

4 Food stylists use a special machine to add sesame seeds to hamburger buns.
a true **b** false

UNIT 9

Seeing the World

WHAT DO YOU ALREADY KNOW?

1 **Think about words you know about tourism and travel. Write the words.**

2 IN PAIRS **Share and compare your information. Add more words to your list.**

Travel and Tourism

DISCUSS & SHARE

VIDEO

3 IN GROUPS **Watch the video and answer the question.**

SYM Is tourism good or bad?

In this unit, you will ...

- talk about travel, make travel recommendations, and give advice on packing.
- use thinking skills: analyze, recall, and infer.
- read about virtual travel.
- use strategies to start and keep talking by taking time to think and asking follow-up questions.
- use collaboration skills to work as a team and create an advertisement to attract tourists.
- learn tips for formal and informal writing.

LESSON 1 Virtual Tours

READING

A **You can go anywhere in the world. Where do you want to go? Discuss as a class.**

B 9.01 **Read the article and choose *True* or *False*.**

There but Not There: Virtual Travel

Would you like to visit another **continent**—Europe, maybe? See Italy or Greece? Or how about a country in Africa, like Kenya? If you want to save time and money when you travel, here's a tip. You need to try virtual tourism! But what is virtual tourism? And how does it work?

When you plan to visit a new place, go online and take a virtual tour first. You can use a virtual reality headset and a computer to take a **tour**. You don't have to use a computer if you have an app on your smartphone.

A virtual tour gives you all the **sights** and **sounds** of a place. Take a tour of a street market in a city like Delhi or enjoy **tourist attractions** in Rio de Janeiro. You can decide what you like to do before you go.

Many people enjoy traveling more when they plan with virtual tours. They like spending time on things that interest them. With virtual tours, they can spend more time on the things they love when they finally get to their dream **vacation** destination!

1 Virtual tourism is only for people with a lot of money. True / False
2 On a virtual tour, you can see and hear a place. True / False
3 You need a computer to take a virtual tour. True / False
4 A virtual tour can help you decide where to go. True / False

C READING SKILL—Scan **Scan the text and complete.**

1 Continents: ______, ______
2 Countries: ______, ______, ______
3 Cities: ______, ______

D THINKING SKILL—Analyze **Answer the questions.**

1 How does a virtual tour save you time and money?
2 Is taking a virtual tour a good idea? Why or why not?

VOCABULARY

A **Match the words and phrases (1–6) to the definitions (a–f). Write the letter.**

1 continent ____
2 sights ____
3 sounds ____
4 tour ____
5 tourist attractions ____
6 vacation ____

a places tourists visit
b a trip around a place to see interesting things
c things you see
d a trip to another place, usually to relax
e large area of land, e.g., North America
f things you hear

GRAMMAR verb + infinitive or gerund

A **Complete with phrases from READING B.**

1 ______ you ______ another continent—Europe, maybe?
2 If you ______ time and money, here's a tip.
3 You ______ virtual tourism!
4 You can decide what you ______ before you go.
5 Many people ______ more when they plan with virtual tours.
6 They ______ time on things that interest them.

B Choose the correct option to complete the grammar rules.

to go = infinitive   *go* = base form   *going* = *–ing* form

1 After *want*, *would like*, *need*, *have*, and *plan*, use the **infinitive** / **base form**.
2 After *enjoy*, use the **infinitive** / **–*ing*** form of verb.
3 After *like*, we can use the **infinitive** / **–*ing*** form of the verb / **both**.

For more practice, go to page 154.

C Write sentences that are true for you.

1 want / don't want … visit Europe / visit Africa
I want to visit Europe. I don't want to visit Africa.

2 would like / wouldn't like … visit a big city / visit a small village

3 like / don't like … travel by boat / travel by bus

4 enjoy / don't enjoy … visit new places / go to places I know

D IN PAIRS Ask and answer questions about your sentences.

A: Do you want to visit Europe?
B: Yes, I do. But I don't want to visit Africa.
A: I want to visit Europe and I want to visit Africa!

PRONUNCIATION *to*

A 9.02 Listen and notice how *to* sounds like /tə/.

I want **to** visit Europe.
Do you like **to** travel?
I don't have **to** work on Monday.

B 9.02 Listen again and practice saying the sentences.

SPEAKING

A Plan a virtual tour.

Where do you want to go? What do you want to see? Choose a place from the unit or use your own ideas.

B Write why you want to visit that place and see that sight in your notebook.
I want to go to Sydney, Australia, and see Bondi Beach because I like to swim.

C IN PAIRS Student A, ask Student B about his or her virtual tour choices. Use phrases and short questions to show you are interested. Then change roles. Use the Confident Communicator box to help you.

Where do you want to go on a virtual tour?
What do you want to do there?

CONFIDENT COMMUNICATOR
KEEP TALKING

Take time to think about what you want to say and how you want to say it. Use words and sounds like:
Um …
Uh …
Let me think …

LISTENING

A IN PAIRS Discuss if you like to visit a place during high tourist season or low tourist season. Write advantages and disadvantages for each.

high season

1 Advantages: good weather, ______

2 Disadvantages: lots of people, ______

low season

3 Advantages: quiet, ______

4 Disadvantages: bad weather, ______

B 9.03 Listen to part of a radio show. Decide whether each speaker prefers high season or low season.

	high season	low season
1 Manuel	☐	☐
2 Andra	☐	☐
3 Viktor	☐	☐

C 9.03 LISTENING SKILL—Listen for detail Listen again and write the words you hear.

1 Manuel: I like the winter, ______.

2 Andra: My favorite time of year is the ______.

3 Viktor: We get tourists all year, but the high season is ______.

D IN PAIRS THINKING SKILL—Recall Two of the speakers prefer the high season. Can you remember the two reasons?

VOCABULARY tourism collocations

A Check (✓) the things you like to do when you visit a place.

1 
☐ buy a souvenir

2 
☐ stay at a hotel

3 
☐ see the sights

4 
☐ take a taxi/bus

5 
☐ take a trip

6 
☐ take a guided tour

B Complete the email with phrases from A.

New Message

From: David Alegre, tour operator — Cc Bcc

To: Erin Rogers — Cc Bcc

Subject: Your trip to our city

Dear Erin,

Thanks for your email and the questions about our city. The high season is December to March. It's a good time to **1** ______________ to the area if you like lots of people. When you come, you can **2** ______________ on Copacabana Beach. There are lots of hotels on the beach. It's a good idea to **3** ______________ around the city with one of our tour guides. That way, you can **4** ______________, such as Sugar Loaf Mountain. If you prefer to explore on your own, **5** ______________ to Corcovado. From there, you can see the city, and of course you can **6** ______________ of your visit there. We look forward to seeing you in our city!

Best wishes,
David Alegre

Send

C Discuss what tourists do when they visit your town or city. Use phrases from A.

GRAMMAR *should/could* for advice and possibility

A Read the sentences from the radio show. Then choose the correct option to complete the grammar rules.

Manuel: Tourists are good for the economy. We should welcome them.
Lucia: We could get more tourists by opening more hotels.

1 Use *should* + **base form of the verb** / **infinitive** to talk about things that are *important* for people to do (advice).
2 Use *could* + **base form of the verb** / **infinitive** to talk about things that are *possible* for people to do (possibility).

For more practice, go to page 154.

B Complete with *could* or *should* and the verb given.

1 You ______________ to China! Or maybe India! They're both interesting. (go / possibility)
2 You ______________ some warm clothes. It can be cold in Sweden! (pack / advice)
3 You need to rest. You ______________ on vacation. (go / advice)
4 Alex ______________ a taxi, or maybe a bus to get downtown. (take / possibility)

C IN PAIRS Make a list of what a good tourist *should* or *could* do in your notebook.

SPEAKING

A IN PAIRS Role-play a conversation. Use the Confident Communicator box to help you.

Student A: You want to take a vacation. Ask questions about your partner's country or city.
Student B: You are a tour operator. Sell a tour to your partner.

A: Hello. I'm going on vacation next summer and I want to visit your country. I want to take a trip, but I don't know where.
B: You could go to … because …

CONFIDENT COMMUNICATOR
KEEP TALKING

There are two ways to make suggestions:
*You **could** take a virtual tour.*
***Why don't you** take a virtual tour?*

VOCABULARY clothes

A Look at the pictures. Write the names of the clothing items using a dictionary.

1	________	**6**	________	**11**	________	**16**	________
2	________	**7**	________	**12**	________	**17**	________
3	________	**8**	________	**13**	________	**18**	________
4	________	**9**	________	**14**	________	**19**	________
5	________	**10**	________	**15**	________	**20**	________

LISTENING

A **IN PAIRS** Ask and answer questions about what you should pack for a short trip to a warm country and a short trip to a cold country.

B **9.04 LISTENING SKILL—Listen for gist** Listen and choose the correct option.

1 José travels **on vacation** / **for work**.
2 Isabela enjoys **swimming** / **hiking** on vacation.
3 Mike likes **swimming** / **hiking** on vacation.
4 Amal likes to visit **beaches** / **cities**.

C **9.04** Listen again and complete. What do the speakers pack?

1 José: ________, ________
2 Isabela: ________, ________
3 Mike: ________, ________
4 Amal: ________, ________

D **THINKING SKILL—Deduce** Match the speakers (1–4) to another destination (a–d). Write the letter. Discuss why it's a good place for him/her.

1 José ____
2 Isabela ____
3 Mike ____
4 Amal ____

a Greenland
b New York
c Chile
d Spain

MAKE IT YOURS

Use a dictionary to find words for clothes that you are wearing now or that you usually wear.

WRITING

A Read the tourism pamphlet. Then think about the climate in your area.

Before you book your trip to Thailand with Thai Tours, we'd like to share some information.

During the cool season (November to February), temperatures in the central region are about 21°C and 14°C in the north. You should pack some warm clothes, such as a sweater or a sweatshirt. During the hot season (March to June), temperatures are between 34°C and 40°C. You need summer clothes, such as shorts, T-shirts, and your swimsuit! The rainy season is from July to October. It's very wet! You should pack a hat and a raincoat.

We look forward to welcoming you to Thailand!

B Plan your writing. Complete the notes for your area.

My area: ______

High-season climate: ______

What to pack: ______

Low-season climate: ______

What to pack: ______

C Write information for tourists visiting your area. Give them advice on what to pack for different times of the year.

SPEAKING

A Look at the different vacations. Choose the one you like best.

1 
an adventure vacation

2 
a beach vacation

3 
a hiking vacation

4 
a sightseeing vacation

B You are going on that vacation! Where are you going? What is the climate like there? Write four things you need to pack for your trip in your notebook.

C IN PAIRS Discuss the trip you are planning. Say what you are taking with you and why. Use the Confident Communicator box to help you.

CONFIDENT COMMUNICATOR
START TALKING

Ask your partner these questions:
What kind of trip are you going on?
Why do you like that kind of trip?
What are you taking with you? Why are you taking that?

Language and Life

Collaboration – Detourism

A 9.05 IN PAIRS **Read the text and discuss the questions.**

DETOURISM

Love or hate it, Venice is a very popular tourist destination. Some people say it's too popular! Around 30 million people visit Venice, Italy, every year. The problem is, they all want to see the same things: the canals, St. Mark's Square, the Doge's Palace. The small city of Venice (population 50,000) attracts large crowds of visitors every year. Tourism is important for the economy of the city, but it's very expensive to keep Venice in good condition.

To deal with this problem, some people suggest detourism. A detour is a short trip in a different direction. Detourism shows tourists attractions that most people don't visit. That way, tourists aren't always in the same place at the same time. For example, when you move away from the canals, Venice also has interesting markets, restaurants, and shops. And there are unusual attractions, such as the multicolored houses on the island of Burano and the Lazzaretto Nuovo, home to the Vampire of Venice! It's a very different side of Venice.

Detourism can lead to many different kinds of vacations and new experiences. Have fun!

Read more

1 What problems does Venice have?

2 What do some people recommend?

B Read the announcement and answer the questions.

TOURISM COMPETITION

Win a weekend vacation for two!

Our area attracts many tourists every year. Most of the tourists are families, but we want to attract more English-speaking young adults to the area, too. We want them to visit our main attractions, but we need to tell them about the many interesting things in our area. Do you have any ideas how to do that? If so, enter the Tourism Competition. You could design a poster, or perhaps you could make a short video. You could also make a slideshow or design a special tour of our area. Choose anything that works for you!

Send your entry to the Local Tourist Office, 135 Main St.

1 What could you win in this competition? ______

2 Who does the Tourist Office want to attract? ______

3 What could you create? ______

C **IN GROUPS** **Decide what you want to create. Choose or add your own ideas.**

a poster
a slideshow
a video
a tour

D **Make a list of tourist attractions in your area. Then choose attractions for your competition entry.**

famous attractions

____
____
____

natural attractions

____
____
____

other attractions (detourism!)

____
____
____

E **Choose three attractions and make notes.**

	Attraction 1	Attraction 2	Attraction 3
What is the attraction?			
What can you do there?			
Why do young adults like it?			

F **Read the advice and create your competition entry.**

TOURISM COMPETITION

Competition entries

A poster
Find some nice pictures of your area. Think about where you want to put the information on your poster. Use topics to interest people.

A slideshow
Find some nice pictures of your area. Use a different slide for each attraction. Include key information. Perhaps include a link to an online video.

A video
Decide who is doing what (such as filming and presenting). Write a short script. Film the tourism video on your smartphone. You can film the attractions!

A tour
Think about some unusual tourist attractions in your area. Think about what young people like to do and see. Write a description of each place on your tour. Find some nice pictures of your area to add to the tour.

G **Share your competition entry with the class.**

MAKE IT DIGITAL

Search online for a detourism tour of a city you are interested in. Tell your class about the tour.

VOCABULARY review

SCORE: / 10

A Complete the definitions with the words in the box.

continent	guided	hotel	scarf	sights
gloves	hat	market	sneakers	souvenirs

1 ________ : you wear these on your hands
2 ________ : you wear this around your neck
3 ________ : you wear these on your feet
4 ________ : you wear this on your head
5 ________ : you buy these on a trip
6 ________ : you stay here on a trip
7 ________ : Africa is an example of this
8 ________ : you see these on a tour
9 ________ : a place to buy things
10 ________ : a type of tour

GRAMMAR review

SCORE: / 10

A Choose the correct option.

Tom: I **1** want / enjoy to visit Ecuador this summer. I **2** enjoy / would hiking and shopping. I **3** have / would like to stay in Quito and visit some small towns as day tours. Is this a good idea?

Ana: I live in Quito, and summer here is very nice. You **4** like / have to visit Otavalo! There's great shopping there. **5** Plan / Want to go on Saturday—the market is very busy then.

B Complete the sentences with *could* or *should* and a word from the box.

eat	go	remember	take	visit

1 I think you ________ Korea in the autumn. It's the best time to visit.
2 There are different ways to get around. You ________ trains, buses, or even planes.
3 You ________ in a big hotel, but think about a small family-run restaurant.
4 Do you like hiking? You ________ to Seoraksan, or maybe Jirisan.
5 Korea can be cold in October. You ________ to pack a jacket.

16–20 correct: You can talk about travel, tourism, and clothes. You can use verb + infinite or gerund and *should/could*.
0–15 correct: Look again at the Vocabulary and Grammar sections in the unit.

TOTAL SCORE: / 20

WHAT DO YOU KNOW NOW? Look back at page 87 and add the words you know now to the box.

STUDY SKILLS FORMAL AND INFORMAL WRITING

Take the quiz about writing skills. Go to **Study Skills** on page 135 to find the answers. Then learn more about formal and informal writing.

1 We often use slang expressions (e.g., *cool, kid, chill out*) in …
a formal writing. **b** informal writing.

2 Which of these sentences is from a formal piece of writing?
a Soccer is a popular sport in Brazil. **b** Soccer is awesome—I love it!

3 Contractions (*I'm, don't, who's*) are usually used in …
a formal writing. **b** informal writing.

4 How do you start a formal letter?
a Dear … **b** Hi …

UNIT 10 Life Stories

WHAT DO YOU ALREADY KNOW?

1 **Think about the last ten photos you took on your phone. Make a list of the photos.**

2 **IN PAIRS Share and compare your photos. Add more words to your list.**

Last 10 photos on my phone

VIDEO

DISCUSS & SHARE

3 **IN GROUPS Watch the video and answer the question.**

SYM How much of your life do you put online?

In this unit, you will …

- talk about life events, social life, and personal experiences.
- use thinking skills: summarize, evaluate, and analyze.
- read about a famous person.
- use strategies to keep talking by showing interest.
- use empathy skills to give advice based on your own experience.
- read about an event organizer to learn about this job and the skills needed for the tourism industry.

A Brave Life

READING

A **Look at the picture. Do you know anything about this person? Why do you think she is famous?**

B 10.01 **Read the biography. Then complete the sentences.**

An Inspiration For All

Malala Yousafzai was born in 1997 in the Swat Valley in Pakistan. Her father was an educator, and he wanted his daughter to get an education, but in 2007 and 2008, the schools for girls closed in her region of Pakistan, and Malala stopped going to school.

Malala wrote a **blog** for British TV about her life that year. She wanted all girls to have the opportunity to get an education. She became **well known** in Pakistan. Then in 2011, Malala's school finally opened again. Malala's blog made some powerful people angry. On October 9, 2012, Malala was shot on her way to school. She was only 14 years old.

Malala was lucky. She survived, and her family took her to England. When she was better, she started school there. She continued to talk about education for girls in Pakistan, and she went around the world to speak. In 2013, she started the Malala Fund. In 2014, she won the Nobel Peace Prize. The next year, a film of her life, called *He Named Me Malala*, told her story. In spring 2017, she went around the world on her Girl Power Trip and met world leaders. She asked them to support education for all girls. In autumn 2017, she started to study for a **degree** at Oxford University.

Malala continues to **inspire** young people around the world.

1 In 2008, Malala's ______________ closed.
2 She wrote ______________ about her life for British TV and became well known.
3 Malala was shot on her way to ______________.
4 She met ______________ when she traveled around the world in 2017.

C **READING SKILL—Scan for information** **Put the milestones of Malala's life in the correct order. Write in your notebook.**

D **THINKING SKILL—Summarize** **Say what happened in Malala's life. Connect your ideas using *then*, *next*, and *after that*.**

MAKE IT YOURS

Find the life story of a person who inspires you. Use a dictionary to find the vocabulary you need to tell his or her life story to the class.

VOCABULARY

A **Match the words and phrases (1–4) to the definitions (a–d). Write the letter.**

1 blog ____
2 well known ____
3 degree ____
4 inspire ____

a a website where people write their opinions
b what you get from a university, for example, Bachelor of Arts
c influence or motivate people
d famous or popular

GRAMMAR simple past (affirmative statements)

A **Read the text in READING B again. Complete with the simple past form of the verbs.**

Regular Verbs

1 start ______________ 2 continue ______________ 3 stop ______________ 4 open ______________

B Complete the table.

Spelling Changes for the Simple Past		
Regular verbs Example: *ask*	Add **1** ____________.	*asked*
Verbs ending in –*e* Example: *live*	Add **2** ____________.	*lived*
Verbs ending in vowel + consonant Example: *stop*	Double the last **3** ________ and add –*ed*.	*stopped*
Verbs ending in consonant + –*y* Example: *cry*	Change *y* to **4** ________ and add –*ed*.	*cried*

For more practice, go to page 155.

C Read the text in READING B again. Write the simple past form of the irregular verbs.

1 have ____________ **2** go ____________ **3** become ____________ **4** meet ____________

D Complete the conversation with the past tense of the verbs.

Logan: Who's that in the picture?

Chase: Oh, that's my grandfather. He **1** ____________ (be) born in 1940. He **2** ____________ (die) a few years ago. He **3** ____________ (have) an interesting life. He **4** ____________ (become) an engineer. He **5** ____________ (start) his own business and **6** ____________ (go) around the world. He **7** ____________ (meet) my grandmother in Spain and they **8** ____________ (marry) in 1970.

PRONUNCIATION the ending *–ed*

A Read the pronunciation rules. How do you think the words are pronounced?

voiced consonant + –*ed* = /d/	unvoiced consonant + –*ed* = /t/	verb ends in *t* or *d* + –*ed* = /ɪd/
learned	stopped	decided

B 10.02 Listen and check. Practice saying the verbs.

SPEAKING

A Write sentences about milestones in your life in your notebook.

B IN PAIRS Discuss. Use the Confident Communicator box to help you.

Choose three milestones and tell your partner about them. Then find another pair and tell them what you learned about each other.

CONFIDENT COMMUNICATOR
START TALKING

To talk about milestones, use *when I was* and your age at the time: *I learned to walk* **when I was** *10 months old.* You can also say the year and then your age: *I graduated from elementary school in 2013, when I was 12.*

Social Life

VOCABULARY social life collocations

A Check (✓) things you did in the last month.

- go out dancing ☐
- have a party ☐
- hang out with friends ☐
- see a movie ☐
- eat out at a restaurant ☐
- go to a concert ☐
- go on a date ☐
- visit family ☐

B IN PAIRS Discuss your social life.

I ate out at a restaurant.
I saw a movie.
I met up with friends and I visited family. And you?

GRAMMAR simple past (negative statements and questions)

A Read the conversation. Underline a negative statement, a *yes/no* question, an information question, and a short answer. Then complete the rules.

Caleb: What did you do last night?
Ryan: I went out with friends. Did you go out?
Caleb: No, I didn't. I didn't want to go out. I stayed home and watched TV.

1 For negative statements, use ______________ + the base form of the verb.
2 For *yes/no* questions, use ______________ + subject + the base form of the verb.
3 For short answers, use *Yes* + subject + *did*, or *No* + subject + ______________.
4 For *wh*– questions, use a question word + ___________ + subject + the base form of the verb.

For more practice, go to page 156.

B Complete the conversation with an affirmative or negative form of the simple past.

Ryan: What **1** ______________ you watch on TV?
Caleb: I watched a movie. **2** ______________ you eat out at a restaurant?
Ryan: Yes, we **3** ______________. We went to Luigi's.
Caleb: What **4** ______________ you have?
Ryan: I **5** ______________ hungry, so I **6** ______________ order a lot. I just had a small pizza.

C IN PAIRS Ask your partner what he or she did last night.

A: What did you do last night? *B: I watched TV.*
A: What did you watch?

LISTENING

A Look at the pictures. What do you think the LISTENING is about?

B 10.03 **LISTENING SKILL—Listen for main ideas** Listen to the conversation. Choose the things that the speakers talk about.

order food	☐	have a party	☐
go on a date	☐	meet up with friends	☐
go out to eat	☐	see a movie	☐
go to a club	☐	visit family	☐

C 10.03 Listen again, and write the reasons each person gives. Then check.

1 Madison: I met up with friends because ______________________.
2 Madison: We went out to eat because ______________________.
3 Luciana: I didn't go out because ______________________.
4 Luciana: I ordered a pizza because ______________________.

D **THINKING SKILL—Evaluate** Is it important to you to have a lot of friends, or do you prefer one or two close friends? Why?

SPEAKING

A Choose a topic to ask your partner about.

what you did last weekend	☐	what you did last summer	☐
the last time you had fun	☐	the last time you found something	☐
the last time you ate out	☐	the last time you forgot something	☐

B **IN PAIRS** Ask each other about your topics. Ask questions to learn more. Use the Confident Communicator box to help you.

C Tell the class what you learned about your partner.

CONFIDENT COMMUNICATOR

KEEP TALKING

To encourage someone to say more:

Really?

Tell me about it. *So, what did you do?*

Tell me more. *Then what happened?*

In My Experience

VOCABULARY collocations with *get*, *have*, and *make*

A Look at the pictures. Write which situations are positive experiences, which are negative experiences, and which can be positive *and* negative.

1 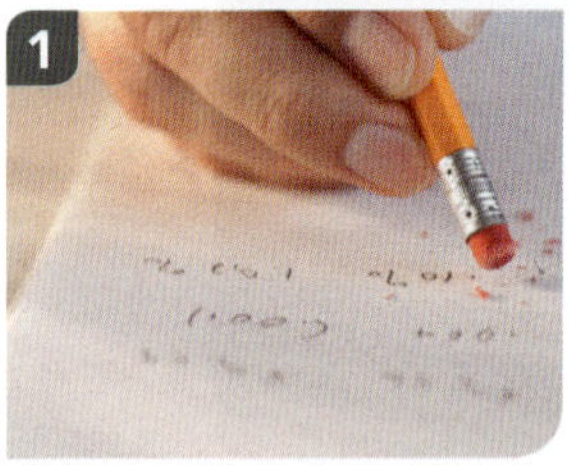
make a mistake ______________

2 
get upset ______________

3 
make a new friend ______________

4 
have an argument ______________

5 
make a decision ______________

6 
have fun ______________

7 
get lost ______________

B Complete the conversation. Use phrases from A.

How was last night? Did you have **1** ______________ at the club?

Yes, we did. But at first Zac and I went to the wrong place! We got **2** ______________!

Oh, no! How did you make a **3** ______________ like that?

I don't know! I thought Zac knew the location. But we didn't get **4** ______________ or have an **5** ______________. We asked a woman and finally found the club. It's a great place!

LISTENING

A 10.04 LISTENING SKILL—Listen for gist Listen and choose the correct option.

1 Kristina is talking about a time when she …
 a forgot something. **b** made a decision. **c** got upset.

2 Javier is talking about a time when he …
 a had an argument. **b** got lost. **c** made a new friend.

3 Lauren is talking about a time when she …
 a had an argument. **b** found something. **c** made a mistake.

B 10.04 Listen again and complete with the words you hear.

1 Kristina: I ______________ it was just a regular party, but it was her birthday, and I ______________!

2 Javier: When I ______________ him, I ______________ him where to go.

3 Lauren: When we ______________ there, they said they ______________ a table for us.

C THINKING SKILL—Analyze Compare the stories in the LISTENING to your life. Did anything like these experiences happen to you? Tell a partner.

WRITING

A Read the email. Choose *True* or *False*.

New Message

From: Juana@email.cc — Cc Bcc

To: avery@email.cc — Cc Bcc

Hi, Avery.

How are things?

The business trip to London was great, but I made a big mistake!

I went to a new restaurant with some friends. We had a good meal, but when we left, a car almost hit me outside the restaurant! I looked left, then right, before I crossed the street. But it's London! You have to look right, then left. Fortunately, the driver stopped in time, but we were both a little scared. He shouted at me to look both ways and drove away.

The next day, I went to the London office and guess what? I met the driver! He's one of my coworkers. In the end, we laughed about our "meeting" the day before. He's a really nice guy.

Write me soon with all your news!

Take care,

Juana

Send

1 Juana liked the restaurant. True / False
2 A car hit Juana. True / False
3 Juana had an argument with the driver. True / False
4 Juana met the driver again later. True / False
5 Juana and the driver are coworkers. True / False

MAKE IT YOURS

Business emails often include some personal experiences. When you describe some of your experiences, you connect with the people you work with.

B Write an email to a friend about a time you made a mistake, got lost, or had an argument. Use *first, next, later,* and *in the end.*

1 When did this happen? ____________________
2 What happened first? ____________________
3 What happened next / later / the next day? ____________________
4 What happened in the end? ____________________

SPEAKING

A Choose one of the experiences and think about a time when it happened to you. What happened? Make notes to help you.

- a time when I got upset
- a time when I had fun
- a time when I lost something important
- a time when I made a new friend

B IN PAIRS Role play. Student A, tell your partner about your experience. Student B, listen carefully to your partner, and ask any questions you have. Then change roles. Use the Confident Communicator box to help you.

CONFIDENT COMMUNICATOR
START TALKING

To say when something happened, use *yesterday, the day before yesterday,* or *last Monday / week / month / year,* etc.
You can also use a period of time + *ago:*
This happened two years ago.

Language and Life

Empathy – Take My Advice

A 10.05 **Read the web page. Then answer the questions.**

THE WORLD ADVICE CORNER

The world's problem-solving web page

Got a problem? Got a solution? Here at the World Advice Corner, we want you to use your experience to help each other. Post your problem and then read the advice from people around the world. Or find a problem and give your advice. Here's a selection of problems on the World Advice Corner.

My problem is that I'm lonely. It's hard to make new friends. I went to a party recently and spent most of the night in the kitchen! I get nervous around people I don't know. Does anyone have any advice? –Adrian

Submit Advice

My parents try to control my life! When I go out with friends, they always want to know exactly where I am and what I'm doing. I have to text them every half an hour or they worry. How can I find a solution? I don't want to argue with them. –Maria

Submit Advice

I have a work problem. Last week, I made a mistake and my boss yelled at me. I got upset and didn't know what to do. Did this ever happen to you? What did you do? All advice is welcome! –Olivia

Submit Advice

1 What happens on the advice website? ____________________
2 What problem does Adrian have? ____________________
3 What problem does Maria have? ____________________
4 What problem does Olivia have? ____________________

B IN GROUPS **Discuss whether you have the same problem. Explain what happened.**

I had the same problem as Olivia. I had an argument with my boss. She said …

C **Read and choose the advice you think best fits each person.**

1 What should Adrian do?
a go to more parties **b** find a hobby **c** play a sport

2 What should Maria do?
a explain how she feels **b** forget her parents and do what she wants **c** ask her parents to explain why they worry

3 What should Olivia do?
a get another job **b** argue with her boss **c** explain to her boss how she feels

D **Make notes on advice for Adrian, Maria, and Olivia.**

I think Adrian should find a hobby because he can meet people with the same hobby.

Adrian: ______________________________

____

Maria: ______________________________

____

Olivia: ______________________________

____

E **IN PAIRS Choose one person from D and write a complete post with your advice.**

Hi, Adrian. It's often hard to make friends, but here's our advice. First, find a hobby you like …

Submit Advice

____

____

____

____

____

F **Share your advice with the class. Take a class vote for the best advice.**

MAKE IT DIGITAL

Find an advice website like the one in the text. Submit a problem you have or one of the problems from **A**. See what advice you receive.

VOCABULARY review

SCORE: / 10

A Match the sentence beginning (1–10) to the sentence end (a–j). Write the letter.

1 Do you want to go on ____
2 Where do you usually meet up ____
3 How often do you go ____
4 At what age did you start ____
5 When did you last ____
6 How do your friends like to have ____
7 What makes you get ____
8 Would you like to watch ____
9 How often do you eat ____
10 In what year were you ____

a make a mistake?
b dancing?
c with friends?
d a date?
e school?
f out at a restaurant?
g a movie?
h fun?
i born?
j upset?

GRAMMAR review

SCORE: / 10

A Complete the paragraph with the simple past form of the verbs in parentheses.

In 2017, 16-year-old student Rayouf Alhumedhi **1** ____________ (write) a text message to a friend. She **2** ____________ (try) to add an emoji, but she **3** ____________ (do not see) any on her phone that she **4** ____________ (like). They **5** ____________ (not look) like her. Alhumedhi, a Muslim from Saudi Arabia, **6** ____________ (want) an emoji with a headscarf. So what **7** ____________ she ____________ (do)? She **8** ____________ (ask) Apple and the Unicode emoji committee to make one. "It's something important to my identity," she **9** ____________ (tell) *Time Magazine*. Apple soon **10** ____________ (have) the new emoji on all its phones.

16–20 correct: You can talk about social life with *get*, *have*, and *make*. You can use the simple past in affirmative and negative statements.
0–15 correct: Look again at the Vocabulary and Grammar sections in the unit.

TOTAL SCORE: / 20

WHAT DO YOU KNOW NOW? Look back at page 97 and add the words you know now to the box.

FOLLOW A PRO EVENT PLANNING

Take the quiz about special events. Go to **Follow A Pro** on page 136 to find the answers. Then learn more about the event planning industry.

1 Social media is the best way to tell people about an event.
a true **b** false

2 How many weddings are there in the US every year?
a 1.2 million **b** 2.4 million **c** 158,000

3 How many birthday cards do people send every year?
a one million **b** one billion **c** two billion

4 40% of couples spend … hours per week planning their wedding.
a 1–5 **b** 5–10 **c** 10–15

UNIT
11 Planning Ahead

WHAT DO YOU ALREADY KNOW?

1 Think of words you know about present and future goals. Write the words.

2 IN PAIRS Share and compare your information. Add more words to your lists.

Present

Future

DISCUSS & SHARE

VIDEO

3 IN GROUPS Watch the video and answer the question.

SYM Do you think of your future or live for now?

In this unit, you will ...

- talk about plans and intentions, ways to save money, and your career goals.
- use thinking skills: apply, calculate, and analyze.
- read about making to-do lists.
- use strategies to keep talking by suggesting alternatives.
- use self-direction skills to make a career plan based on your interests.
- learn tips about personal development.

READING

A Which statement is true for you? Check (✓) and explain.

I use to-do lists every day. I need them to organize my time! ☐
I sometimes use to-do lists when I have a lot of things to remember. ☐
I never use to-do lists. I keep it all in my head! ☐

B 11.01 Read the article and discuss the question.

1 What mistake do people make with to-do lists?

WHAT TO DO ABOUT TO-DO LISTS

What are you going to do today?

Maybe you're going to write an important email, shop for a gift, or make a dentist **appointment**. We all have busy lives and it's easy to **forget** things we're supposed to do.

A list of things to do—or a "to-do list"—helps us **remember** what to do, but many people make a big mistake when they write their lists: they list a lot of things and then only do half of them. Here are some tips for writing a useful to-do list.

1 Write three things you are going to do in one day. Choose the things that are really important and write your list the night before. That way, you're **ready** to go in the morning!

2 When you have more than three things to do, write the top three and do them first. Then make a new list and write another three things. If you have one big job to do, break it into smaller jobs.

3 Write exactly what you need to do. Don't write "learn English." Write "learn eight new English words." People do things on their lists when it's **clear** what to do.

4 Be ready to change your list. Things are going to happen that you didn't **plan**. When they do, write a new list. Life is full of surprises!

C READING SKILL—Read for the main idea Choose the main idea of the text.

1 We should use to-do lists more.
2 To-do lists can be very helpful if you follow some basic tips.

D THINKING SKILL—Apply Write your to-do list for tomorrow. Follow the advice in the text. Compare lists with a partner.

VOCABULARY

A Complete with the words from the box.

appointment	clear	forget	plan	ready	remember

1 I have my phone and my money. I'm ______________ to go!
2 Things on your list should be ______________ and easy to understand.
3 I have a/an ______________ to see the doctor on Monday.
4 When you ______________ something on your list, you don't do it.
5 Did you ______________ to call your mom?
6 I ______________ to go shopping with friends on Saturday.

GRAMMAR *going to*

A **Underline the sentences with *going to* in the article from READING B.**

B **Read the sentences you underlined. Complete the rule.**

1 Before *going to*, we use the verb ____________ in the correct form.
  a *be* **b** *have* **c** *do*

2 After *going to*, we use the ____________ of the verb.
  a base form **b** *–ing* form **c** infinitive

3 We use *going to* to talk about plans and ____________.
  a offers **b** requests **c** predictions

For more practice, go to page 157.

C **Read and complete the plans (1–2) and predictions (3–4).**

1 A: What are you going to do this weekend?
  B: Oh, ______________________________! (see my cousins)

2 A: Do you and your friend have any plans for tonight?
  B: Yes! ______________________________. (go dancing)

3 A: What do you think about your exams?
  B: I'm really worried. I think ______________________________! (fail)

4 A: It's a beautiful day!
  B: Yeah … but ______________________________. (get cold later)

D **IN PAIRS Discuss the questions.**

1 What are you going to do tonight? What else is going to happen then?
2 What are you going to do this weekend? What else is going to happen then?

PRONUNCIATION *going to*

A **11.02 Listen and notice how the speakers say *going to*. *Going to* is often pronounced /gʌnə/. Practice saying the dialogues in GRAMMAR C.**

SPEAKING

A **Do you agree or disagree with the predictions? Then add your own prediction.**

	Strongly agree	Agree	Not sure	Disagree	Strongly disagree
1 More education is going to help me get a job.	☐	☐	☐	☐	☐
2 I'm going to own a successful business before I'm 30.	☐	☐	☐	☐	☐
3 My career is going to change a lot in the next five years.	☐	☐	☐	☐	☐
4 ______________________________	☐	☐	☐	☐	☐

B **Choose a statement you agree with in A. Write a plan to help your prediction come true.**

I'm going to own a successful business before I'm 30. I'm going to start my own online business …

C **IN PAIRS Talk about your predictions and plans. Use the Confident Communicator box to help you.**

CONFIDENT COMMUNICATOR
START TALKING

To ask about future plans, say: *What are you going to do?* To ask about future plans at a specific time in the future, say: *What are you going to do* + time expression, e.g., *What are you going to do tomorrow / next month / in December?*

Saving for the Future

VOCABULARY money

A Match the opposites. Write the number (1–6).

1

buy ____

2

spend ____

3

sell ____

4

rich ____

5

save ____

6

poor ____

B IN PAIRS Discuss the questions.

1 Do you save money every month or do you spend all of it?
2 What was the last thing you bought? What was the last thing you sold?

LISTENING

A Look at the picture. What do you think the person in the picture is doing? Why is he doing that?

B 11.03 LISTENING SKILL—Listen for specific information
Listen and match each person (1–2) to the reason why they want to save money (a–b). Write the letter.

1 David ____ a to rent an apartment
2 Patricia ____ b to go on vacation

C 11.03 Listen again and choose *True* or *False*.

1 David earns a lot from his job. True / False
2 He spends a lot of money on rent. True / False
3 He is going to save money on food. True / False
4 Patricia wants to spend money on expensive gifts. True / False
5 She made a photo album for her mom. True / False
6 She wants her brother to make her a pizza. True / False

D THINKING SKILL—Calculate Estimate how much you can save doing what David and Patricia are going to do.

MAKE IT YOURS

Make a list of things you spent money on this month. Then make a list of ways you could save money next month.

GRAMMAR direct and indirect objects

A Read and complete the rules.

David: This month, I'm going to make sandwiches for myself.
Patricia: I'm going to make him pizza!

1 In "make sandwiches for myself," *sandwiches* is the direct object. What is the indirect object?
____

2 In "make him pizza," *pizza* is the direct object. What is the indirect object? ____________

Some verbs can take a direct object and an indirect object. Notice the word order.

3 subject + verb + direct object + preposition + indirect object
People give gifts ____________ *each other.*

4 subject + verb + indirect object + direct object
People give each other ____________.

5 Use the preposition ____________ with the verbs *give, bring, sell, send, show,* and *tell.*

6 Use the preposition *for* with the verbs *buy, cook,* and *make.*

For more practice, go to page 157.

B Rewrite the underlined phrases. Do not use a preposition.

Money-saving tips

Why don't you <u>make a gift for your friend</u> for her birthday?

1 ____

You could <u>cook a meal for your family</u> and save on eating out.

2 ____

You could <u>buy local food for a visitor</u> as a souvenir of his visit.

3 ____

When your friends have a party, why not <u>bring homemade cookies for them</u>?

4 ____

C IN PAIRS Write two more money-saving tips in your notebook. Use two of the verbs from A.

SPEAKING

A Make a list of reasons for saving money in your notebook.

B Role-play a conversation. Student A, you want to save money for a nice birthday gift for a family member. Tell your partner why you want to save money and ask him or her how to save money. Student B, suggest ways Student A could save money. Use the Confident Communicator box to help you.

CONFIDENT COMMUNICATOR
KEEP TALKING

To suggest alternatives, use *You could …* e.g., *You could make lunch at home.* You can also use negative questions with *Why don't you …?* e.g., *Why don't you make a gift?*

LESSON 3 Career Plans

VOCABULARY career plans collocations

A Check (✓) the things you want to do in your future career.

1 
☐ work outdoors

2 
☐ manage people

3 
☐ work in an office

4 

☐ start a business

5 
☐ work from home

6 
☐ work overseas

B IN PAIRS Discuss your future career plans. Use phrases from A.

I want to work for a large company. I'm probably going to manage other people. I also want to work overseas …

LISTENING

A IN PAIRS What do you need to do to get your dream job? Discuss.

B 11.04 LISTENING SKILL—Listen for gist Listen and make notes on Jade's advice.

How to get your dream job:

First, ____

____

Second, ____

____

Finally, ____

____

C THINKING SKILL—Analyze Decide what other advice is useful for getting your dream job.

- Talk to people with the job you want.
- Network with family and friends.
- Volunteer at places with similar jobs.
- Go to job fairs.
- other: ____

WRITING

A Read the journal entry. Underline sentences with *so* and *because*.

Saturday, May 15

It's time to think about my career, so I need to set some goals and make a plan. In the next two years, I'm going to start my own business because I want to be the boss. I know a lot about cooking, so I want to open my own restaurant!

I need to learn more about cooking and food safety, so I'm going to study at a culinary college that teaches those things. Then, I'm going to take a business course. I have to understand money and business to run a restaurant.

And finally, I'm going to practice cooking because I need to improve my skills!

Well, that's my plan!

FOLLOW

B Choose the correct phrases to complete the rules.

1 Use *so* to talk about the **result of** / **reason for** something.
2 Use *because* to explain the **result of** / **reason for** something.

C Complete the career plan with your own goals.

In my future career, I'm going to ____________________

So, I'm going to ____________________

____

because ____________________

____

D Write a journal entry describing your career plans in your notebook.

SPEAKING

A Make notes to answer the questions.

1 What is your dream job? ____________________
2 What are you going to do to get that job?
learn a skill   do an internship   get a degree/certificate
____
3 Do you think you will use English in your dream job? How?
____

B IN PAIRS Discuss your career plans and if English is important for your dream job. Use the Confident Communicator box to help you.

CONFIDENT COMMUNICATOR
REPAIR IT

When you aren't sure about what you are saying, at the start of your sentence, say: *I guess* or *I suppose*.
I guess I'm going to use English with people on the phone.

Language and Life

Self-direction – From Hobby to Career

A 11.05 **Read the article. Answer the questions.**

Follow Your Passion

15. Oct 11:24

Many of us have a hobby or a free-time activity we love, but is it possible to make that hobby a career? For some people, the answer is "yes." Love baking? Start a cake-making business. Exercise every day? Start a career as a personal trainer. Today, lots of people are finding that social media can help them turn their passion into a career.

Fiorella Pia has an interesting hobby. She takes photographs of food and shares them on a social networking website. She has a talent for making the food look nice. She has a lot of followers and her pictures are very popular. Now she wants to turn her hobby into a career. She wants to earn money from her photography. She's going to plan carefully. She needs to decide exactly what kind of business to start. She also needs to write a business plan. She's asking all her friends for their advice as she puts together her career plan.

Read more

1. Which hobbies can become careers, according to the article? ____________
2. What is Fiorella's hobby? ____________
3. What does she want to do now? ____________

B IN GROUPS **Make a list of careers that involve photography. Then compare your lists as a class. Which group thought of the most careers?**

wedding photographer

photojournalist

____

____

C Read the information. Then decide what Fiorella's A/B/Z choices should be.

When you are making a career plan, it's a good idea to have "A/B/Z" choices. Reid Hoffman, founder of LinkedIn, created the A/B/Z plan. An "A" choice is your dream choice. This is the career you really want. You need a bit of luck to get it, but this is your dream career.

Your "B" choice is your alternative plan. This is the choice for when Plan A doesn't work out. It isn't your dream career, but it is close.

Your "Z" choice is an emergency choice. This is what you can do when Plan A and Plan B don't succeed. Perhaps you can do this for a short time and think about a new Plan A/B.

Fiorella Pia's Career Plan:

1 A choice: ____________________
2 B choice: ____________________
3 Z choice: ____________________

D IN GROUPS Discuss the different goals Fiorella should have. Make a list of clear short-term, mid-term, and long-term goals.

Short-term goals (up to 1 year):

do 3 or 4 weddings as a photographer and build a website

____

____

Mid-term goals (1–5 years):

employ one assistant and rent a studio

____

____

Long-term goals (5 years +):

employ photographers and open studios in three major cities

____

____

E IN PAIRS Ask and answer questions about your choices and suggestions.

1 Explain your A/B/Z choices for Fiorella.
2 Say what you think her short-, mid-, and long-term goals should be.

F IN PAIRS Discuss the questions.

1 Do you have a hobby that could become a career?
2 What could you do to make money from your hobby?
3 Is it always a good idea to make a career out of a hobby? Are there any possible problems?

MAKE IT DIGITAL

Go online and find careers related to your favorite hobby. Make a list of your A/B/Z choices.

VOCABULARY review

SCORE: / 10

A Complete the conversation with words from the box.

appointment business luck manage overseas ready remember saved sell skills

Nate: Excuse me. Ms. King? I'm Nate West. We have a 2:30 **1** ____________.
Ms. King: Of course, I **2** ____________. Have a seat. So, tell me about yourself, Nate.
Nate: Well, right now I work part-time in a café. I'm good with money and **3** ____________ people well. I think these are good **4** ____________. I **5** ____________ some money from my job, so after I graduate, I plan to work **6** ____________ for a year, maybe in Colombia.
Ms. King: Why is that?
Nate: You see, I'd like to start a **7** ____________ someday. I want to **8** ____________ coffee to cafés. But I'm not **9** ____________ to do that now. First, I need to learn about growing coffee. I think with a little **10** ____________, it can be a big success.

GRAMMAR review

SCORE: / 10

A Complete the sentences with the correct form of *be going to* and the verb in parentheses.

1 Greg and Lisa ____________ (get) married on Sunday.
2 My brother is sick, so he ____________ (not go) to work today.
3 ____________ you ____________ (visit) me this weekend?
4 Where ____________ your sister ____________ (go) after work?
5 My mother and father ____________ (spend) the weekend with me.

B Choose the correct option.

1 Ken and Zoe's wedding is this weekend. Let's buy a special gift for **him** / **it** / **them**.
2 Mr. Green doesn't feel well. Why don't we make **us** / **him** / **it** some chicken soup?
3 Can you give **it** / **me** / **you** a campus tour? I'm new here.
4 Mrs. Ortega's company wants to send **it** / **her** / **she** to Moscow for three weeks.
5 Your parents are in town? Do you plan to cook dinner for **him** / **her** / **them**?

16–20 correct: You can talk about to-do lists, money, and career plans. You can use *going to*, direct and indirect objects.
0–15 correct: Look again at the Vocabulary and Grammar sections in the unit.

TOTAL SCORE: / 20

WHAT DO YOU KNOW NOW? Look back at page 107 and add the words you know now to the boxes.

STUDY SKILLS PERSONAL DEVELOPMENT

Take the quiz about time management. Go to **Study Skills** on page 137 to find the answers. Then learn more about time management.

1 **… of business and professional people regularly write to-do lists.**
a 20% **b** 40% **c** 70%

2 **Around … of students feel stressed every day.**
a 49% **b** 68% **c** 99%

3 **The average person uses … different methods to manage their time.**
a 3 **b** 7 **c** 13

4 **Students who do their work at the last minute get … students who finish their work early.**
a better grades than **b** worse grades than **c** the same grades as

UNIT 12

The Great Outdoors

WHAT DO YOU ALREADY KNOW?

1 Think of words you know about the weather, climate, seasons, and natural features where you live. Write the words.

2 IN PAIRS Share and compare your words. Add more words to your lists.

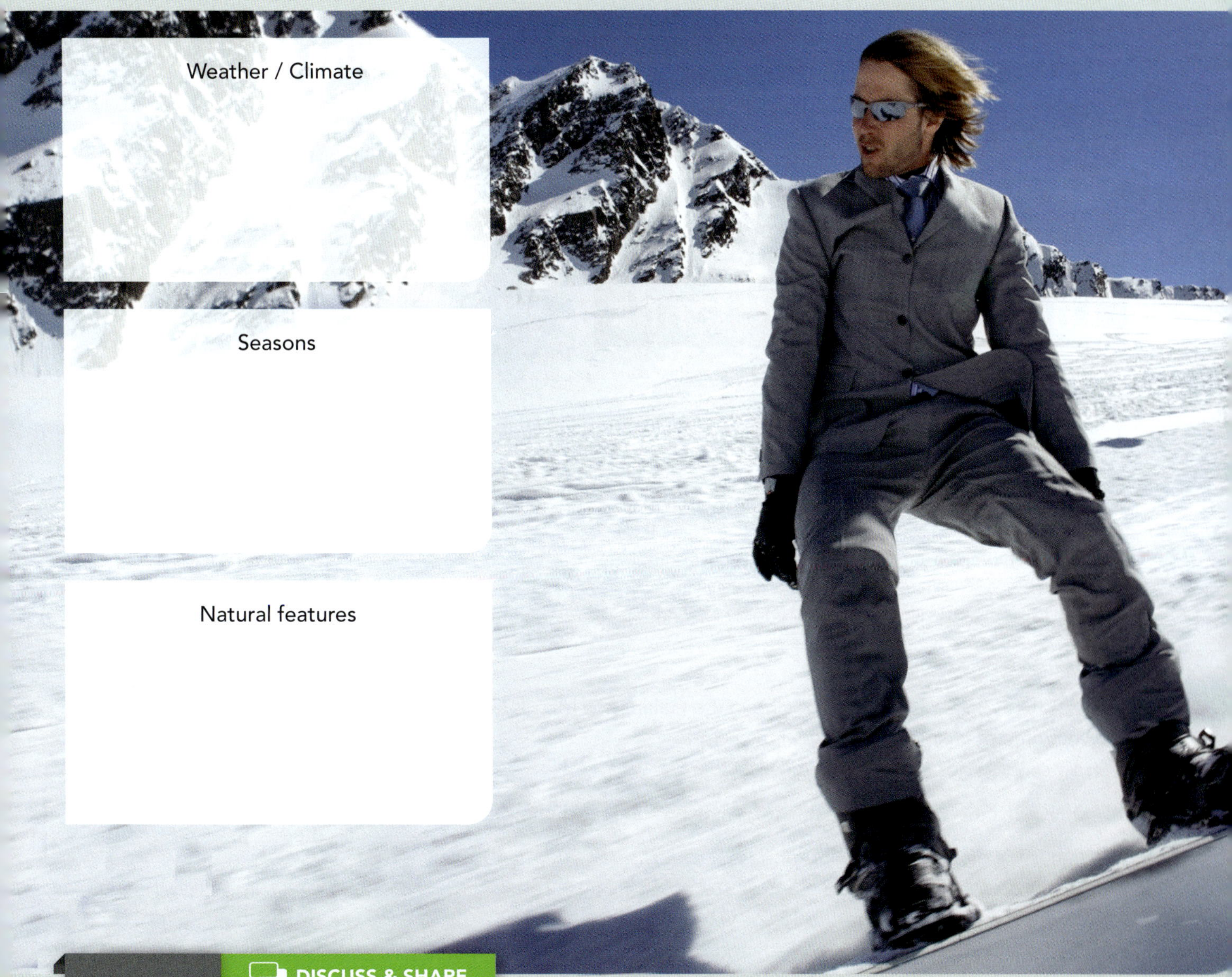

Weather / Climate

Seasons

Natural features

VIDEO

DISCUSS & SHARE

3 IN GROUPS Watch the video and answer the question.

SYM Are you an adventurer?

In this unit, you will …

- talk about climate, weather, natural features, and outdoor activities.
- use thinking skills: infer, hypothesize, and recall.
- read about the Galapagos Islands.
- use strategies to keep talking by showing interest.
- use problem-solving skills to decide how to develop a natural area.
- read about a forest ranger to learn about this job and the skills needed for the environmental field.

READING

A Look at the pictures in the brochure in B. Answer the questions.

1 What are the people in the photographs doing?
2 Do you enjoy these kinds of activities?

B 12.01 Read the brochure. Answer the questions.

The Galapagos Islands

The Galapagos **Islands** are an amazing place for a tour. There are beautiful sandy beaches, awesome animals, and the people are friendly. Every year, new people learn what the Galapagos Islands have to offer. People can swim, dive, and see nature—the Galapagos have it all!

The islands are near the **equator**. They don't have seasons like some other places do, but there is a **cool** season from June to November. The water is colder at that time, and there's less rain, so it's drier. It's a great time for diving around the islands. It's also a good time to see whales, sea lions, and penguins. The **temperature** is around 21–27°C, and the water is around 18–24°C.

From December to May, the temperature is higher. It's called the warm season. It's more **tropical** during these months, and the skies are cloudier. It's also wetter than the rest of the year. The ocean is warmer and it's better for swimming. It's also a good time to see iguanas, flamingos, and other tropical birds. The temperature is around 27–32°C. The water is cooler than that, at around 21–26°C.

To get there, you need to go to Ecuador. From Ecuador, you can fly to Baltra Island or San Cristóbal Island, or go by boat. Of course, it's quicker to fly than go by boat. Flights are also cheaper, but then you have to pay for a hotel. A luxury cruise ship is more expensive than a trip on a small boat.

1 What time of year is better for diving in the Galapagos Islands?
2 What time of year is better for swimming?
3 How can you get to the Galapagos Islands?

C READING SKILL—Scan for specific information Read and complete.

1 What is the air temperature in April? ______________
2 Is it wet or dry in September? ______________
3 When is the water temperature 18–24°C? ______________
4 When is a good time for seeing flamingos? ______________

D THINKING SKILL—Understand Answer the questions.

1 What time of year is there more rain in the Galapagos Islands?
2 Why don't the Galapagos Islands have spring, summer, fall, and winter?

MAKE IT REAL

Most countries use the Celsius scale to measure temperature. For 27–32°C, we say "twenty-seven to thirty-two degrees Celsius." A few countries, including the United States, use Fahrenheit (F).

VOCABULARY

A Complete with words and phrases from READING B.

1 These are areas of land that have water around them. ______________
2 This is an imaginary line around the center of the Earth. ______________
3 This describes weather that is not very hot, or a little cold. ______________
4 This tells you how hot or cold a place is. ______________
5 This describes weather that is very hot and wet. ______________

GRAMMAR comparative adjectives

A Read the text in READING B again. Underline the comparatives.

The water is colder and there is less rain, so it's drier.

B Complete the table with the examples.

Most one-syllable adjectives	Add *–er*: *long–longer, cold–* **1** __________, *quick–* **2** __________
One-syllable adjectives ending in *–e*	Add *–r*: *nice–nicer, rare–rarer*
One–syllable adjectives ending in consonant–vowel–consonant	Double the final consonant and add *–er*: *hot–hotter, wet–* **3** __________
One- or two-syllable adjectives ending in *–y*	Change the *y* to *i* and add *–er*: *dry–* **4** __________, *happy–happier*
Adjectives with two or more syllables	Use *more* or *less*: *interesting–more/less interesting, expensive–* **5** __________
Irregular adjectives	*bad–worse, good–* **6** __________

When comparing two things directly in the same sentence, use *than*: *Today is hotter than yesterday.*

For more practice, go to page 158.

C Complete the text using the comparative form of the words given. Add *than* if needed.

Peru has three different regions: the coast, the Andes, and the rain forest. They all have different climates. The coast is **1** __________ (cool) the other two regions, with average temperatures of 18°C in Lima in August. The weather is **2** __________ (warm) in February, with average temperatures of 27°C.

In the Andes, the weather is **3** __________ (wet) from September to May, and **4** __________ (dry) from June to August. The Andes is **5** __________ (sunny) the coastal area.

The rain forest is **6** __________ (rainy) the coast and the Andes. It is also **7** __________ (hot), with average temperatures of 30–32°C all year round.

SPEAKING

A Research the climate of a country or city you are interested in. Write down the temperature and weather at different times of the year.

B IN PAIRS Student A, you want to visit your friend. Ask about the weather in your friend's country or city at different times of the year. Student B, tell your friend about the weather in your country or city at different times of the year. Then change roles. Decide where you both would like to go on a trip, and when. Use your notes and the Confident Communicator box to help you.

CONFIDENT COMMUNICATOR
KEEP TALKING

To learn about a place, say: *What's it like?*
To ask about weather, say: *What's it like in summer?* or *What's it like in February?*

Natural Features

VOCABULARY natural features

A **Check (✓) the natural features you can find less than 100 kilometers (60 miles) from where you live.**

desert

forest

hill

lake

mountain

river

volcano

waterfall

B **IN PAIRS Name examples of each natural feature in your country.**

An example of a waterfall here in Chile is the Laja Falls.

LISTENING

A **Look at the picture. Where do you think this place is?**

MAKE IT YOURS

Can you think of more natural features in your country? Find out what they are called.

B **12.02 Listen and choose *True* or *False*.**

1 Kerry is a student. True / False
2 The Iguazu River starts in Argentina. True / False
3 Niagara Falls is just one waterfall. True / False
4 The speaker went to Angel Falls last year. True / False

C **12.02 LISTENING SKILL—Listen for specific information Listen again and complete the table.**

	Country	Height	Number of waterfalls	Good time to visit
Iguazu Falls			300	
Niagara Falls	Canada/US	50 meters		
Angel Falls				May–October

D **THINKING SKILL—Induce Answer the questions.**

1 Which of the waterfalls do you want to see? Why?
2 How do you think people feel when they visit places like Iguazu Falls?

GRAMMAR review of tenses

A Match the sentences. Write the letters.

1 I love waterfalls because **I'm studying** geology in college and waterfalls are great places to learn more. ____
2 When it gets to the border with Argentina, **it falls** 82 meters. ____
3 Last year, **I went to** the Iguazu Falls in Argentina and Brazil. ____
4 **I'm going to** visit Angel Falls next May because the water is higher then. ____

a This is a single action in the past.
b This is a future plan.
c This is true in the present.
d This is generally true.

For more practice, go to page 159.

B Complete with the correct form of the verbs from the box.

feel go (×2) have learn love stay

Two months ago, I **1** ____________ to the White Mountain National Forest in Maine. The forest **2** ____________ many hiking trails and lakes. I **3** ____________ there for a week and camped. It **4** ____________ great to be outdoors, under the stars at night. I **5** ____________ how to catch fish right now. Next time I go to Maine, I **6** ____________ swimming in the lakes. Nature is very important to me. I **7** ____________ the outdoors!

C Play a game of *True or False?* Write two things that are true about you and one thing that is false. Use the time expressions. Ask your partner to guess if your statements are true or false. Take turns.

Last year, I … *Right now, I …* *Next month, I …*

Last year, I flew on a plane. Right now, I'm learning the piano. Next month, I'm going to visit my cousin in the US.

SPEAKING

A Think of a natural place you enjoyed visiting. Make notes on what you know or what you want to find out about it.

Place: ____________________

Facts: ____________________

____

B Make notes on what happened when you went there. How did you feel there?

____

____

C IN PAIRS Discuss. Tell your partner about the place you visited. Use your notes from A and B. Use the Confident Communicator box to help you.

CONFIDENT COMMUNICATOR
KEEP TALKING

When someone tells a story, we can respond using the phrases:
That's very interesting!
That sounds really good/bad.
How interesting/wonderful/sad!

Wonders of the Natural World

VOCABULARY adjectives to describe natural features

A Circle the positive adjectives and underline the negative adjectives.

amazing attractive awesome beautiful boring fantastic popular ugly

B Choose three places. Say what you know and think about them. Explain.

I think the Grand Canyon is awesome! It's beautiful and I want to see it one day.

THE SEVEN NATURAL WONDERS OF THE WORLD

Mount Everest, Himalayas, China/Nepal

Grand Canyon, Arizona, US

Great Barrier Reef, Australia

Parícutin Volcano, Mexico

Aurora Borealis, near the Arctic

Harbor of Rio de Janeiro, Brazil

Victoria Falls, Zambia/Zimbabwe

PRONUNCIATION /ju/

A 12.03 Listen and notice. The long *u* sound /u/ sometimes has a *y* sound /ju/.

beautiful communicate cute document music popular

B Practice saying the words with the correct pronunciation.

LISTENING

A 12.04 Look at the phrases and guess the natural wonder. Then listen to check.

... it appeared in a corn field ...

... it grew very quickly ...

... local people take visitors ...

... on horseback ...

B 12.04 LISTENING SKILL—Listen for detail Listen and answer the questions.

1 When did it appear? ______________
2 How can you get to the small town near the volcano? by ______________ or ______________
3 How can you get to the volcano from the town? ______________
4 How can you get to the top of the volcano? ______________
5 How long is the complete trip? ______________

C THINKING SKILL—Recall Tell a partner what you learned about the volcano. Do you want to visit the volcano? Why or why not?

WRITING

A Read the guidebook entry and check (✓) the information the writer mentions.

HAKONE, JAPAN, is a town with many hot springs. Hot springs are places with natural hot water that comes up from the ground. The Hakone hot springs are very popular with local people and tourists. You can relax in the hot water and enjoy the amazing natural views. Hakone is about 90 minutes from Tokyo by train. It is close to the famous Mount Fuji. You can take a train to Odawara Station and then take a bus. Hakone is 20 minutes by bus from the train station. There are many hotels in Hakone if you want to stay for a few days. You can also go on a tour of the area. Search "Hakone hot springs" online for more information.

- who enjoys this place ☐
- what you can do here ☐
- where it is ☐
- how to get there ☐
- how much the train costs ☐
- where to stay ☐
- where to learn more ☐

B Choose a local natural feature you know. Answer the questions.

1. What place are you going to write about? ______
2. Why is it interesting or attractive? ______
3. What can you do there? ______
4. Where is it? How can you get there? ______
5. Can you stay there? Where? ______
6. Is there a website with more information? ______

C Write a guidebook entry for young adults from other countries. Use your answers in B to create your entry.

SPEAKING

A Choose an outdoor activity to talk about. Make notes to answer the questions.

1. Where can you do this activity in your area?

______

2. What do you like about this activity?

______

3. Is there anything you dislike about this activity?

______

MAKE IT YOURS

Some guidebooks ask people to write about their local area for tourists. Do you know any examples of guidebooks like that? What do you think is interesting about guidebook writing?

B IN PAIRS Talk about the outdoor activities in A. Use the Confident Communicator box to help you.

CONFIDENT COMMUNICATOR
KEEP TALKING

When you are listing points (e.g., things you like about an activity), you can use *One thing I like about it is …* and *Another thing I like about it is …*

***One thing I like about camping** is that you sleep under the stars!*
***Another thing I like about it is** it's really quiet at night.*

Language and Life

Problem-solving – Developing a Natural Area

A 12.05 **Read the newspaper article. Answer the questions.**

LOCAL COLLEGE ASKS FOR IDEAS by Janice Baskin

Meadowville College is a college near our city. There is a large lake and a forest on Meadowville's campus. Right now, not many people use the lake or the forest. Some people go swimming or camping there in the summer.

Recently, the college decided to use this area for its students. Dean Linda Collins says, "We want our students to learn about nature and learn new skills. Many of our students come from big cities and they don't know a lot about nature. They are more familiar with technology than they are with the natural world." The college wants students to be interested in nature. "They need activities to introduce them to outdoor life. Maybe something that uses technology can get them interested—something that connects nature to their studies," says Dean Collins.

The college is asking students for ideas and suggestions. They have money for the project and they are happy to spend it on the right ideas.

1. Where are the lake and the forest? ____________________
2. What do people do there right now? ____________________
3. What does the college want students to learn? ____________________
4. Why don't some students know much about nature? ____________________
5. What does the college want from students? ____________________

B IN GROUPS **Read the statements from students. Talk about the ideas and check (✓) the ones you think are good suggestions.**

1. What about an app with useful information about the natural features on campus? ☐
2. They should buy boats and tents and leave us to explore the area on our own. ☐
3. We need an information center where we can learn about the natural history. ☐
4. They should get instructors to teach courses on swimming and camping. ☐
5. Other: ____________________ ☐

C **IN PAIRS** **Choose one of the ideas. Answer the questions.**

- [ ] **Relaxation**
  They should make quiet, relaxing areas where students can chat and study on their own.
- [ ] **Sports**
  They should build a sports center and have instructors offer classes for different outdoor sports or activities.
- [ ] **Technology**
  They should create a mobile app that gives useful information to get people interested in exploring the area.
- [ ] **Nature**
  They should build a center where students can learn about the wildlife and history of the area.

1 What are the main points that support your idea?

____

____

____

2 What is the main point against your idea?

____

____

____

3 What do you say to argue that point?

____

____

____

D **Take turns. Explain your ideas to the class. Give reasons.**

We think the college should build a nature center. It can even have art classes, so students can paint pictures of nature.
Also, …

E **Take a vote with your class. Choose the idea you like best. Don't vote for your own idea.**

MAKE IT DIGITAL

You are going to post your idea on the college website. What information should you give about your idea? What images should you use?

VOCABULARY review

SCORE: / 10

A Choose the correct option.

There are many boats on the **1 desert / river**. Boat tours are very **2 ugly / popular**.
People left cans and bottles at the top of the **3 mountain / forest**. **4** It was **ugly / awesome**.
The **5 island / volcano** looked red and orange at night. The colors were **6 beautiful / boring**.
I walked in the **7 forest / waterfall** all day. I had so much fun. It was **8 amazing / boring**.
I swam in a lake under the **9 forest / waterfall**. It was **10 fantastic / attractive**!

GRAMMAR review

SCORE: / 10

A Read the information. Then complete the sentences with the comparative form of a word in the box. Add *than*.

expensive high long hot wet

The Mississippi River: 3,734 m / The Mekong River: 4,350 m
Yearly rainfall in Chicago: 93 cm / Yearly rainfall in Boston: 111 cm
Hotels in Istanbul: \$120–\$130 / Hotels in Panama City: \$130–\$140
Mt. Blanc: 4,808 m / Mt. Fuji: 3,776 m
Miami: 32°C / Montreal: 24°C

1 The Mekong River is ______________________.
2 Boston is ______________________.
3 Hotels in Panama City are ______________________.
4 Mt. Blanc is ______________________.
5 Miami is ______________________.

B Complete the paragraph with the correct form of the verb in parentheses.

Every year my friend Wendy and I **1** ______________ (take) a two-week vacation. We're in Belize right now. The sun **2** ______________ (shine) and we're on a beautiful beach. I **3** ______________ (learn) how to scuba dive now. Tomorrow we **4** ______________ (dive) in the famous Blue Hole. I **5** ______________ (learn) about this in one of my classes last year.

16–20 correct: You can talk about natural features and adjectives to describe them. You can use comparative adjectives.
0–15 correct: Look again at the Vocabulary and Grammar sections in the unit.

TOTAL SCORE: / 20

WHAT DO YOU KNOW NOW? Look back at page 117 and add the words you know now to the boxes.

FOLLOW A PRO NATURAL SCIENCE

Take the quiz about careers in natural science. Go to Follow A Pro on page 138 to find the answers. Then learn more about careers in natural science.

1 How many gardeners and florists say they are happy in their job?
a 52% **b** 79% **c** 87%

2 Spending … outside gives your brain as much energy as drinking one cup of coffee.
a 10 minutes **b** 20 minutes **c** 1 hour

3 Nearly half of all jobs need some kind of outdoor work.
a true **b** false

4 One park ranger, Roy Sullivan, lived through seven lightning strikes and … bear encounters in his 40-year career.
a 22 **b** 7 **c** 13

UNIT 7

STUDY SKILLS

A Read the conversation. On a scale of 1–5, rate the group work (1 = no communication, 5 = excellent communication).

EFFECTIVE GROUP WORK

Amy So, we don't have very much time to get our presentation on Australian culture ready. Are you listening, Marco?

Marco Um, yes—I'm just reading about Australian art …

Amy What artists do you want to talk about?

Marco I don't know yet. Sorry—I didn't read the book.

Amy Well, let's …

Tammi Hey, guys! Sorry I'm late! The traffic is bad today.

Amy Oh, that's okay. So, Marco—you're reading about Australian art. Can you talk about that for about two minutes? And can you talk about music, Tammi?

Tammi I'm not sure … I don't know very much about …

Marco And what are *you* doing for the presentation, Amy?

Amy Um … well, I don't know yet. I'm still thinking …

Marco Can you talk about food?

Amy No, I don't want to do that …

Tammi The sports teams?

Amy No, that's a terrible idea. What are you doing, Roberto? You're very quiet!

Tammi So, am I doing food, then?

B Check (✓) the reasons the group is not working well together.

- ☐ One student is late.
- ☐ One student wants to work alone.
- ☐ One student isn't well prepared.
- ☐ One student isn't saying anything.
- ☐ One student is negative about the other students' ideas.
- ☐ One student is talking on the phone to a friend.
- ☐ One student is giving jobs to other people but isn't doing any work.

C Match the tips about group work (1–5) to the expressions (a–e). Write the letter.

Tips	Expressions
1 Include all members of the group. _____	a Why don't we find some old pictures?
2 Say when you agree with someone's idea. _____	b Sara, what do you think?
3 Make suggestions. _____	c I think that's a really good idea!
4 Be positive about other people's ideas. _____	d Yes, I agree with you.
5 Share what you know. _____	e I read an interesting blog post about that …

D Rewrite the conversation in A. Show how a group can work together well. Use the language in C to help you.

Amy: What are we doing for our presentation?
Marco: I'm reading a book on Australian art. Can I do something about that?

E THINKING SKILL—Understand Describe how teamwork is important in the workplace. What jobs need teamwork?

✓ MAKE IT HAPPEN

Prepare a group presentation on a famous English-speaking person. Decide what to present and how to do the work. Remember to work as a team!

A: Let's do a presentation on Abraham Lincoln. He's an interesting man.

B: I have a good book about Abraham Lincoln.

Answers to the quiz on page 76
1 a 2 b 3 a 4 b

UNIT 8

FOLLOW A PRO

A **Read about a food stylist's job. Answer the questions below.**

A FOOD STYLIST

The photos of food in magazines, cookbooks, restaurant websites, and travel guides always look so good. Do you know why? It's because a food stylist works to make the food look amazing in pictures. And that's what I do. I'm Alfonso Garcia, and my job is to make food look real when it's not. For example, do you know that a bowl of strawberry ice cream isn't really ice cream? It's mashed potato! Ice cream melts very quickly in a hot studio, so we use pink mashed potato instead. And here's a disgusting idea—we put motor oil on meat to make it look delicious and hot! I love my job, but I can't eat the food I work with. It all goes in the trash can!

1 What does a food stylist do? ______
2 What do food stylists use instead of strawberry ice cream? Why? ______
3 Why do food stylists put motor oil on meat? ______
4 What happens to the food that Alfonso uses? ______

B **Discuss the questions as a class.**

1 How important is a food stylist's job?
2 Think about places where you see pictures of food. How does the food look?
3 Would you like to be a food stylist?

VIDEO

WATCH THE VIDEO AND FOLLOW A BAKER.

C **IN GROUPS Answer the questions.**

1 What job is the video about? ______
2 Where does the person work? ______
3 Is the person's job difficult? Why or why not? ______
4 What skills does the person need for the job? ______
5 Does the person work long hours? ______
6 What doesn't the person like about the job? ______

D **IN GROUPS Check your answers to the quiz on page 86 and discuss the questions.**

1 What different food industry jobs can you think of?
2 Which food industry job sounds most interesting to you?
3 What qualifications do you need to work in the food industry?
4 What skills and abilities do you need to work in the food industry?
5 What are the good and bad points about working in the food industry?

Answers to the quiz on page 86
1 a 2 a 3 a (to make it look fat)
4 b (They add the seeds by hand.)

STUDY SKILLS

A **Read the two texts. Which one is formal and which one is informal? Why?**

FORMAL VS. INFORMAL WRITING

Text 1

Corsica is an island on the south coast of France. The population is 330,000. The official language is French. Every year, more than three million people visit Corsica. Most people come in summer, when the weather is usually hot (the average temperature is 22°C, according to Météo France). It is warm and dry all year round.

In Corsica, you can swim in the sea and go to the beach. A lot of people go walking in the hills or visit the historical buildings. Sant'Antonino is a very old village in the northeast of Corsica. It goes back to the 9th century and is a popular place for tourists to visit.

Text 2

I love Corsica! I go to Corsica every year with my family and we always have a good time. It's a really cool place because it's so beautiful. The sea is very blue and the weather is always good—it never rains! The people are friendly, too, and there are lots of cafés and markets where you can find great fruit, cheese, and meat. Go there if you can! 🙂

B **Write *Text 1* or *Text 2* for each sentence.**

1. The writer uses sources with facts and data. ______
2. The writer doesn't give a personal opinion. ______
3. The writer says how he or she feels. ______
4. The writer uses contractions (e.g., "it's" instead of "it is"). ______
5. The writer groups ideas together in paragraphs. ______
6. The writer uses an emoji. ______

C **Write whether the sentences are *Formal* or *Informal*.**

1. Over 800 million people around the world do not have clean drinking water. ______
2. I think that's so sad! ______
3. It's a cool place to visit. ______
4. First, we need to think about why this happens. ______
5. I wanna try and answer that question. ______
6. According to the *Daily Morning Times* news, hundreds of young people are going overseas to find work. ______

D **Rewrite the informal sentences in C so that they are formal and rewrite the formal sentences so that they are informal.**

E **THINKING SKILL—Analyze** **Compare and contrast when you have to write formally and when you can write informally. What happens if you write formally in an informal situation?**

✓ MAKE IT HAPPEN

Write a formal paragraph about a country. Do some research online to find out facts about that country.

Panama is a country between Central and South America. It has a population of around four million. It is famous for the Panama Canal, which connects the Atlantic and Pacific Oceans.

Answers to the quiz on page 96
1 b 2 a 3 b 4 a

UNIT 10

FOLLOW A PRO

A **Read about an event organizer. Answer the questions below.**

AN EVENT ORGANIZER

Dale Langdon started Star Events, Inc. four years ago. He loves social events, and he likes to help people celebrate special times in their lives. It's not easy to organize a wedding for 300 people or an 80th birthday party for a large family, but Dale does that every day. Each event starts with a meeting. People tell Dale what kind of event they want and how many people they want to invite. Dale asks questions to find out more about the person's ideas. Dale then makes sure it all happens. He has to find a place for the event and make all preparations for the event—from the music to the parking. For some events, he has to find musicians, photographers, dancers, chefs, DJs, and servers. It's a lot of work, but Dale likes it.

1 Why did Dale start Star Events, Inc.? ______
2 What kind of events does Dale organize? ______
3 What does each event start with? ______
4 How does Dale find out what people want? ______
5 What services does Dale need to find? ______

B **Discuss the questions as a class.**

1 What do you think is enjoyable about this career?
2 What do you think is not enjoyable about this career?
3 Imagine you are an event organizer. A young woman wants an unusual event for her 21st birthday. Money isn't a problem. What do you suggest?

VIDEO

WATCH THE VIDEO AND FOLLOW A TOUR GUIDE.

C **IN GROUPS** **Answer the questions.**

1 Where does the person work? ______
2 What does the person do every day? ______
3 What does the person say is the best part of the job? ______
4 What skills does the person need? ______
5 Who does the person work with? ______

D **IN GROUPS** **Check your answers to the quiz on page 44 and discuss the questions.**

1 What different events do people need help with planning?
2 Which events take the most time and money to plan?
3 What personal qualities do you need to work in the events industry?
4 Are there opportunities for this job where you live?
5 Do you need English for this job?

Answers to the quiz on page 106
1 a 2 b 3 c 4 c

UNIT 11

STUDY SKILLS

A Read the conversation. Is Maria a good time manager?

PERSONAL DEVELOPMENT

Sally Hey, Maria! What are you doing?
Maria Hi, Sally! I'm writing a schedule.
Sally Why?
Maria Well, I have a lot of work to do, and it's important that I don't forget things. For example, I have a math test next month.
Sally But that's next month! You don't need to think about that now.
Maria I do! It's important to plan now so I don't rush at the last minute.
Sally Are you going to study for two hours every day? That's too much.
Maria Well, I don't know how long I need to study. So it's better to give it two hours in the schedule.
Sally What does it say here? "Relax"? Why are you writing that?
Maria It's important to have time for myself. If I work too hard, I can't focus.
Sally Oh, I see. And why are you coloring it in?
Maria I color the things that are really important red, like my math test, for example. If it's not so important, then it's green.
Sally "Sally's birthday." Ah, thank you, Maria. But hey … why are you coloring that in green?

B Choose *True* or *False*.

1 Maria is making a schedule because she has a lot to remember. **True / False**
2 Maria is writing her math test in her schedule at the last minute. **True / False**
3 Maria is sure she needs to study math for two hours every day. **True / False**
4 Maria doesn't want to relax because she wants to focus on her studies. **True / False**
5 Maria colors in things so she doesn't forget them. **True / False**

C Match the tips about managing your time (1–5) to the reasons (a–e). Write the letter.

1 Plan time to relax and do something you enjoy. _____
2 Write down due dates in your calendar. _____
3 Decide what is very important and not very important in your to-do list. _____
4 Write down every important task you need to do. _____

a Then you can do the important things first.
b If you feel better, you work better.
c That way you don't forget about it.
d Then you can see how long you have to complete the task.

D IN PAIRS Role-play. Student A: You are having problems managing your time. Student B: Give Student A advice about managing his or her time.

Ula: I'm so stressed! I have two exams this week, and I have no time to study!
Tony: Don't worry. Maybe I can help you …

E THINKING SKILL—Predict What can happen if you don't manage your time well at school or work? Are you good at managing your time? Why or why not?

MAKE IT HAPPEN

Make a schedule for the next week. Talk with a partner about the ways you can manage your time.

Answers to the quiz on page 116
1 c 2 a 3 c 4 b

UNIT 12 FOLLOW A PRO

A **Read about a forest ranger's job. Answer the questions below.**

A FOREST RANGER

Forest rangers usually work in national parks and areas of natural beauty. The job can be more dangerous than other jobs, but it's also more enjoyable than an office job for many people. Most rangers in the United States of America work for the Forest Service.

Forest rangers have many jobs. In the summer, when the weather is hotter, they need to prevent fires. They talk about the dangers of forest fires. They tell tourists and schoolchildren about fire safety. They sometimes cut down trees to stop fires. They help firefighters if there's a fire in the forest.

Forest rangers make sure people are safe outdoors. They give information about hiking trails. They teach people how to be safe when camping or hiking in the forest, and how to stay safe from bears and other wild animals. They also help rescue people if they get lost or if things go wrong.

1 Where do forest rangers usually work? __________
2 What do they talk to tourists and children about? __________
3 Why do forest rangers cut down trees? __________
4 What do forest rangers teach people to do? __________

B **Discuss the questions as a class.**

1 Why is being a forest ranger sometimes a dangerous job?
2 Would you like to work outdoors all the time? Why or why not?
3 What can you do to prevent a fire?

VIDEO

WATCH THE VIDEO AND FOLLOW A BOTANIST.

C **IN GROUPS Answer the questions.**

1 What is the person's job? __________
2 Where does the person work? __________
3 What skills does the person need for the job? __________
4 Does the person like the job? Why or why not? __________
5 Who does the person work with? __________

D **IN GROUPS Check your answers to the quiz on page 64 and discuss the questions.**

1 Do you know anyone who works outdoors in nature?
2 What different outdoor jobs do you know?
3 What physical abilities do you need to work outdoors?
4 What are the challenges of working in nature?
5 What skills do you need to work in nature?

Answers to the quiz on page 126
1 c 2 b 3 a 4 a

Irregular Verbs

Infinitive	Simple past	Past participle
be	was/were	been
become	became	become
begin	began	begun
break	broke	broken
bring	brought	brought
build	built	built
buy	bought	bought
catch	caught	caught
choose	chose	chosen
come	came	come
cost	cost	cost
cut	cut	cut
do	did	done
draw	drew	drawn
drink	drank	drunk
drive	drove	driven
eat	ate	eaten
fall	fell	fallen
feed	fed	fed
feel	felt	felt
find	found	found
fly	flew	flown
get	got	gotten
give	gave	given
go	went	gone
grow	grew	grown
hang	hung	hung
have	had	had
hear	heard	heard
hit	hit	hit
hold	held	held
hurt	hurt	hurt
keep	kept	kept
know	knew	known
leave	left	left
let	let	let
lose	lost	lost
make	made	made
meet	met	met
pay	paid	paid
put	put	put
read	read	read
ride	rode	ridden
ring	rang	rung
rise	rose	risen
run	ran	run
say	said	said
see	saw	seen
sell	sold	sold
send	sent	sent
set	set	set
sing	sang	sung
sit	sat	sat
speak	spoke	spoken
stand	stood	stood
stick	stuck	stuck
take	took	taken
teach	taught	taught
tell	told	told
think	thought	thought
throw	threw	thrown
understand	understood	understood
wake	woke	woken
wear	wore	worn
win	won	won
write	wrote	written

Pronunciation Symbols

Vowels

ɪ	did
ɛ	bed
æ	bad
ʌ	cup
ʊ	book
ə	banana
i	feed
ɑ	father, box
ɔ	tall
u	student, food
ɝ	shirt, birthday
eɪ	date, table
aɪ	cry, eye
ɔɪ	boy
oʊ	comb, post
aʊ	about, how

Consonants

p	park, happy
b	back, hobby
t	tea
d	die
k	came, kitchen, quarter
g	game, go
f	face, photographer
v	vegetable
θ	thing, math
ð	then, that
s	city, summer
z	please, goes
ʃ	she, shop
ʒ	leisure
h	hot, who
tʃ	chicken, watch
dʒ	jacket, orange
m	men
n	sun, know
ŋ	sung, singer
w	week, white
r	rain, writer
l	light, long
j	yes, use, music

Grammar Review

A Match the sentence beginning (1–8) to the sentence end (a–h). Write the letter.

1 What's your name? _____
2 Is he your father? _____
3 Where are you from? _____
4 How old is she? _____
5 Are you and Jill from Canada? _____
6 Is her name Maria? _____
7 Who's that? _____
8 Are they Colombian? _____

a I'm from Mexico.
b No, we're not.
c That's Etsuko.
d Yes, he is.
e No, they're not.
f My name's Greg.
g Yes, it is.
h She's 18.

B Look at the picture. Complete the sentences with the words from the box.

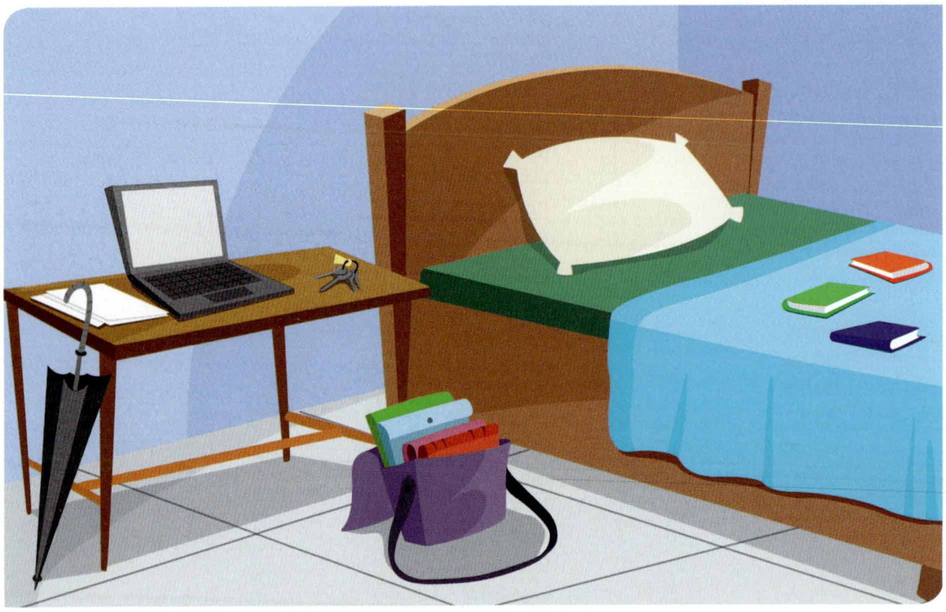

a an any are is isn't aren't some

1 There __________ a small bed.
2 There __________ any pens on the desk.
3 There __________ a laptop on the bed.
4 There __________ some keys on the desk.
5 There's __________ bag in front of the desk.
6 There aren't __________ chairs.
7 There's __________ umbrella next to the desk.
8 There are __________ books on the bed.

C Complete the sentences with the correct form of the verb in parentheses.

1 She __________ (work) in a large office in Chicago.
2 They __________ (not work) on weekends.
3 I __________ (take) the number 6 bus to school.
4 We __________ (not live) near the train station.
5 Our school __________ (have) a great cafeteria.
6 He __________ (not go) to work by subway.

D **Write the questions. Add *do* or *does* in the correct place.**

1 you / wear a uniform / ? ___
2 where / they / go / after work / ? ___
3 your teacher / drive / to school / ? ___
4 that bookstore / sell / notebooks / ? ___
5 how / I / get to / the bus station / ? ___
6 who / she / study with / on weekends / ? ___

E **Rewrite the sentences with the words in parentheses.**

1 They are late for class. (often) ___
2 I do laundry at night. (sometimes) ___
3 My sister cleans the house. (hardly ever) ___
4 Mr. Sanchez works on Saturday. (usually) ___
5 We are at the office by 9:00. (always) ___
6 They go shopping on weekends. (never) ___

F **Choose the correct option.**

1 Eric is a good singer, but he **can't to dance** / **cannot dancing** / **can't dance** at all.
2 I **am can speak** / **can speak** / **can speaks** two languages—Spanish and English.
3 Where **do I can get** / **can I get** / **can I to get** some coffee?
4 **Can you play** / **Do you can** / **Can you playing** the piano?
5 She **can't drive** / **can't drive** / **can't drives** a car.
6 What sports **can you play** / **is it can play** / **can't you played** well?

G **Complete the sentences about what is happening right now. Use the words in parentheses.**

1 Kevin ___ (read) a book.
2 Alex and Jan ___ (not feel) well.
3 Mark and I ___ (play) a video game.
4 It ___ (rain).
5 Those students ___ (not listen).
6 The teacher ___ (check) our work.
7 It ___ (not snow).
8 You ___ (work) very hard.

H **Choose the correct option.**

Ana: Let's make **1 a** / **some** list before we go shopping.

Will: Good idea. So, what do we need?

Ana: Let's see … well, we don't have any **2 vegetables** / **vegetable**, so let's get **3 some** / **any** tomatoes and carrots.

Will: OK. And I want to make **4 an** / **some** omelet for breakfast. Do we have **5 an** / **any** eggs?

Ana: Um … yes, we do.

Will: How **6 many** / **much**?

Ana: Just two, so let's get some. And how about I make cheeseburgers for dinner?

Will: Sounds great! How **7 many** / **much** beef do you want?

Ana: Half a kilo. And don't forget the cheese. We don't have **8 any** / **some**.

UNIT 7 — *can/can't* (ability)

Function

We use *can/can't* to talk about ability. We use the same form for all nouns and pronouns (*I can sing. / He can sing.*).

Form

Statements		***Yes/no* questions**	**Answers**
I You We They He She	can ride a bicycle. can't drive a car.	Can you sing? Can she take good pictures?	Yes, I can. / No, I can't. Yes, she can. / No, she can't.
		Information questions	**Answers**
		What musical instrument can you play? How many languages can he speak? Where can we get Mexican food?	I can play the piano. He can speak three languages. You can get it at Rosa's Café.

A Choose the correct option.

1 Birds **can** / **can't** fly.
2 Babies **can** / **can't** run.
3 Children **can** / **can't** sing.
4 Fish **can** / **can't** swim.
5 Animals **can** / **can't** talk.
6 Computers **can** / **can't** be helpful.

B Complete the sentences about what the people can (✓) and can't (X) do.

	speak Portuguese	**play tennis**	**drive a car**
Mark	X	✓	✓
Beth	✓	✓	X
Todd	X	X	✓

Mark **1** ____________ play tennis and **2** ____________. Todd **3** ____________, but he **4** ____________ speak Portuguese or **5** ____________. Beth **6** ____________ ____________, but she **7** ____________ ____________ and **8** ____________.

UNIT 7 — adverbs of manner

Function

We use adverbs of manner to describe actions. They go after the main verb. Add *–ly* to an adjective to form an adverb (*quick–quickly*). There are some irregular adverbs (*fast–fast, hard–hard, good–well*).

Form

Adjective	**Adverb**
They are noisy eaters.	They eat noisily.
He is a fast runner.	He runs fast.
She is a good dancer.	She dances well.

A Choose the correct form of the word.

1 She is singing **beautiful** / **beautifully**.
2 They speak English **good** / **well**.
3 He's a **slow** / **slowly** runner.
4 They're **quiet** / **quietly** neighbors.
5 Please pass the ball **careful** / **carefully**.
6 I'm learning these new rules **easy** / **easily**.

B Complete each sentence with the adverb form of the adjective in parentheses.

1 Bend your knees ______________. (slow)
2 They don't swim very ______________. (fast)
3 He sometimes speaks ______________ (angry) to me.
4 She plays the piano ______________. (good)
5 Please put the glass down ______________. (gentle)
6 Don't throw the ball ______________. (hard)

UNIT 8 — countable and uncountable nouns

Function

Countable nouns are things and people we can count. They can be singular (*apple*) or plural (*apples*). Uncountable nouns are people or things we can't count. They don't have a plural form (*milk*). We use *How many …?* with countable nouns and *How much …?* with uncountable nouns.

Form

Countable nouns		Uncountable nouns
Singular	**Plural**	
I have a banana. We need an egg.	I have three bananas. We need some eggs.	I want some tea. We need some orange juice.
	How many apples are there?	How much bread is there?

A Write C (*countable*) or U (*uncountable*) for each noun.

1 vegetables _____
2 beef _____
3 water _____
4 grape _____
5 noodles _____
6 potato _____
7 bread _____
8 sugar _____
9 melon _____
10 rice _____
11 carrot _____
12 flour _____

B Choose the correct option.

1 How **many** / **much** milk do we have?
2 **Is** / **Are** there butter in the fridge?
3 Do you have **an** / **some** orange?
4 You need to add **a** / **some** salt.
5 There **is** / **are** some onions in this dish.
6 How **many** / **much** people are at the party?

UNIT 8 — *this/that/these/those*

Function

We use *this/these* to talk about things near us. We use *that/those* to talk about things not near us. We use *this/that* for singular and uncountable things and *these/those* for plural things.

Form

Singular	Plural
This soup is delicious. That restaurant is a 15-minute drive away.	These melons weigh five kilograms each. Those people across the park can't hear us.

A Look at the pictures. Complete the sentences with *this, that, these,* or *those*.

1 How much are ____________ donuts?

2 Can I please have ____________ basket?

3 Is ____________ black jacket on sale?

4 Are ____________ bananas from Peru?

B Choose the correct option.

1 Is this / that your cup of coffee over there? I think it's getting cold.
2 Look at these / those directions here. I don't understand them.
3 Can you hold this / that box for me? It's really heavy and my arms hurt.
4 Who are these / those people in the other room? Do you know them?

UNIT 9 — verb + infinitive or gerund

Function

Some verbs (e.g., *want*, *need*, and *plan*) are followed by an infinitive (*to* + verb). Some verbs (e.g., *enjoy*) are followed by a gerund (verb + *–ing*). Some verbs (e.g., *like*) are followed by either an infinitive or a gerund, with no change in meaning.

Form

Verb + infinitive	**Verb + gerund**
I want to travel to Mexico. He would like to take a guided tour. She needs to get a passport. We have to buy some souvenirs. They plan to take a vacation soon.	I enjoy traveling by boat. **Verb + infinitive or gerund** They like to visit new cities. They like visiting new cities.

A Find and correct one error in each sentence.

1 She wants get a hotel near the city center. ______
2 Do you need get a new backpack for your trip? ______
3 I don't enjoy to travel in a large group. ______
4 They plan spending two weeks in Thailand. ______
5 He doesn't like to eating in hotel restaurants. ______
6 Would you like visit Europe or Asia? ______

B Read the travel blog. Complete the sentences with the infinitive or gerund form of the verb in parentheses.

I'm here in Oaxaca, Mexico! This city is great. I am enjoying **1** ______ (walk) around the city very much, but tomorrow I plan **2** ______ (take) a guided tour of the market. I want **3** ______ (try) some local food. I like **4** ______ (meet) the local people, but my Spanish is not very good. I really need **5** ______ (study) the language more. I have **6** ______ (buy) some cool souvenirs for my family, and I would like **7** ______ (get) a good price.

UNIT 9 — *should/could* for advice and possibility

Function

We use *should* to give advice to others and *could* to say what is possible for people to do. Both are followed by the base form of a verb (e.g., *should stay, could visit*).

Form

***should* + verb (advice)**
Everyone needs a passport to go overseas. You should get one right away. It's very cold and snowy there right now. You should pack a warm coat.
***could* + verb (possibility)**
There are lots of places to stay. You could stay in a hotel, at a hostel, or with a local family. All the islands in Hawaii are popular. You could visit Oahu, Maui, Kauai, or the Big Island.

A Match the sentence beginning (1–6) to the sentence end (a–f). Write the letter.

1 Don't take a suitcase on your trip. You should ____
2 I hear you like cold weather. You could ____
3 It's very hot there right now. You should ____
4 I want to follow you on your trip. You should ____
5 You don't drive? You could ____
6 Not many people speak English. You should ____

a post updates every few days.
b plan to stay out of the sun.
c take a taxi or a bus to the airport.
d learn some of the local language.
e visit Iceland, Alaska, or even Siberia!
f bring just a small backpack.

UNIT 10 — simple past (affirmative statements)

Function

We use the simple past to talk about states, events, and actions in the past.

Form

We generally add *–ed* to regular verbs (e.g., *walk–walked, live–lived, stop–stopped*).

Regular verbs	**Add *–ed*.**	**listen–listened**
Verbs ending in *e*	Add *–d*.	love–loved
Verbs ending in vowel + consonant	Double the last consonant and add *–ed*.	hop–hopped
Verbs ending in consonant + *y*	Change *y* to *i* and add *–ed*.	copy–copied

There are many irregular simple past forms (e.g., *speak–spoke*, *take–took*, *eat–ate*). See the irregular verbs chart on page 71. Notice spelling patterns on the list of irregular verbs.

Affirmative statements	
I You He She It We They	inspired many people. had an interesting life.

A Write the simple past forms of the verbs.

1 eat ____
2 learn ____
3 play ____
4 speak ____
5 talk ____
6 become ____
7 do ____
8 have ____
9 cry ____
10 shop ____
11 make ____
12 go ____

B Write the simple past forms of the verbs.

Look at this picture of my parents. My father was born in Mexico. He **1** ____________ (come) to the US in 1990. He **2** ____________ (work) in Texas for many years. He **3** ____________ (meet) my mother in 1995. They **4** ____________ (get) married two years later. They **5** ____________ (start) a family and **6** ____________ (have) me in 1999. Later they **7** ____________ (move) to California and **8** ____________ (open) a small restaurant. They **9** ____________ (buy) their first home in 2007.

UNIT 10 — simple past (negative statements and questions)

Form

We use *didn't* (*did not*) + the base form of the verb to form negative simple past statements (*didn't work, didn't go, didn't say*). To ask *yes/no* questions, we use *Did* + subject + the base form of the verb (*Did you live there?*). For short answers, we use *Yes* + subject + *did* or *No* + subject + *didn't* (*Yes, we did. / No, we didn't.*). To ask information questions, we use a *wh–* question word + *did* + subject + the base form of the verb (*Where did they grow up?*).

Negative statements		*Yes/no* questions	
I You He She It We They	didn't work hard. didn't have an easy life.	Did you like the story? Did they tell anyone?	Yes, I did. / No, I didn't. Yes, they did. / No, they didn't.
		Information questions	
		What did you talk about? Where did he grow up? Who did they see?	I talked about you. He grew up in Germany. They saw their grandparents

A Complete the sentences using the negative simple past form of the verbs.

1 They woke up early. They ____________ late.
2 We felt very cold. We ____________ very hot.
3 She had a big family. She ____________ a small family.
4 It seemed like a good idea. It ____________ like a bad idea.
5 I lived in a noisy neighborhood. I ____________ in a quiet neighborhood.
6 He gave a short speech. He ____________ a long speech.
7 We bought an old house. We ____________ a new house.
8 I read an interesting book. I ____________ a boring book.

B Complete the conversation with short answers or the simple past form of the verbs in parentheses.

Diego: **1** ____________ your family ____________ (come) to visit you last weekend?
José: Yes, they **2** ____________ (do). I **3** ____________ (show) them around the city.
Diego: Where **4** ____________ you ____________ (go)?
José: To the beach. But they **5** ____________ (not enjoy) it much.
Diego: **6** ____________ you ____________ (take) them to eat out?
José: No, I **7** ____________ (not do). They **8** ____________ (want) to cook for me. I **9** ____________ (not mind)!

UNIT 11 — *going to*

Function

We use *going to* to talk about future plans and predictions.

Form

Affirmative statements	*Yes/no* questions and short answers	
I'm going to take a summer class. She thinks she's going to fail her exam.	Are you going to stop by later? Is he going to visit his family?	Yes, I am. / No, I'm not. Yes, he is. / No, he isn't.
Negative statements	**Information questions**	
We're not going to travel this summer. It's not going to be very sunny today.	Where are you going to study? When is she going to see Matt?	In London. This winter.

A Complete the conversations with the correct form of *going to* and the verbs in parentheses.

1 A: What **1** ______________ you ______________ (do) this weekend?
B: I'm not sure. I think I **2** ______________ (clean) the house.

2 A: **3** ______________ the weather ______________ (be) nice tomorrow?
B: No, it isn't. It **4** ______________ (rain) all day.

3 A: Gina **5** ______________ (not work) on the project with me.
B: Oh, no! **6** ______________ anyone ______________ (help) you?

4 A: When **7** ______________ your parents ______________ (visit)?
B: On Friday. They **8** ______________ (spend) the weekend with me.

5 A: **9** ______________ you and Rex ______________ (get) married?
B: Yes, we are, but we **10** ______________ (not have) a big wedding.

UNIT 11 — direct and indirect objects

Function/Form

Some verbs take both an indirect object (often a person) and a direct object (often a thing).

Subject	Verb	Indirect object	Direct object
I He	am going to make sent	her us	a cake. a nice gift.

When the direct object comes first, we need to add the preposition *for* for the verbs *buy, cook,* and *make* and the preposition *to* for the verbs *bring, give, send, sell, show,* and *tell*, before the indirect object.

Subject	Verb	Direct object	Preposition	Indirect object
I He	am going to make sent	a cake a nice gift	for to	her. him.

A Complete the sentences with the words in parentheses. Put the indirect object first.

1 Sorry, but I didn't give ______________________________. (your message / Maggie)
2 They aren't going to show ______________________________. (me / their new car)
3 Can you please show ______________________________? (your new home / us)
4 Gregory is going to buy ______________________________. (his wife / a surprise gift)
5 We want to make ______________________________. (a nice dinner / you)
6 Are you going to bring ______________________________? (your mother / flowers)

B Rewrite the sentences. Put the direct object first.

1 I gave him the letter. ______________________________
2 I didn't buy her a gift. ______________________________
3 Let's cook your parents dinner. ______________________________
4 I want to show you something. ______________________________
5 She sold me her used car. ______________________________
6 I'm going to make you some soup. ______________________________

UNIT 12 — comparative adjectives

Function

We use comparative adjectives to compare two people or things. We use *than* after the adjective (e.g., *The Pacific Ocean is bigger than the Atlantic Ocean.*).

Form

Use	Example
For most one-syllable adjectives, add *–er*.	warm–warmer quick–quicker
For one-syllable adjectives ending in *–e*, add *–r*.	nice–nicer wide–wider
For one-syllable adjectives ending in consonant + vowel + consonant, double the final consonant and add *–er*.	red–redder wet–wetter
For one-syllable adjectives ending in consonant + *y*, and for two-syllable adjectives ending in *y*, change the *y* to *i* and add *–er.*	dry–drier sunny–sunnier
For most other adjectives with two or more syllables, use *more* or *less* + adjective.	more expensive less interesting
Some adjectives have irregular comparative forms.	good–better bad–worse
Some one-syllable adjectives use *more* and *less*.	fun–more fun, less fun

A Write the comparative form for the adjectives.

1 large ____________
2 hot ____________
3 happy ____________
4 bad ____________
5 beautiful ____________
6 easy ____________
7 near ____________
8 windy ____________
9 big ____________
10 important ____________
11 thin ____________
12 good ____________

B Write one sentence that compares two things. Use the adjective in parentheses and add *than*.

1 Mt. Kilimanjaro > Mt. Etna (high)

____

2 the Atacama Desert > the Gobi Desert (dry)

____

3 Iceland > Spain (cool)

____

4 the Amazon River > the Mekong River (wide)

____

5 a plane ticket > a bus ticket (expensive)

____

6 an A+ grade > a C– grade (good)

____

UNIT 12 — review of tenses

Function/Form

Use	Example
We use the simple present to talk about likes, dislikes, preferences, habits, and routines.	I like traveling in a small group. Martin goes camping every summer.
We use the present progressive to talk about things that are happening now.	I'm waiting for the rain to stop. Cindy is updating her blog right now.
We use the simple past to talk about states, events, and single actions in the past.	I went to Costa Rica last year. Hannah hurt her ankle on the hike.
We use *going to* to talk about plans and predictions.	I'm going to visit Iguazu Falls next year. It's going to start snowing soon.

A Complete the paragraph. Use one of the four tenses in the chart and the verb in parentheses.

I **1** ____________ (love) to travel. I **2** ____________ (go) to a different place every year. Last year, my friend and I **3** ____________ (visit) the Grand Canyon, in Arizona. We **4** ____________ (fly) to Las Vegas and then **5** ____________ (take) a bus from there. We **6** ____________ (spend) five days at the canyon. Right now, I **7** ____________ (think) about my next trip. I am **8** ____________ (go) to Arizona again. I **9** ____________ (want) to see Monument Valley. I am **10** ____________ (drive) there. Many tourists **11** ____________ (visit) this amazing place every year.

Unit 7

Track 01

New Gadget Reviews

Are you looking for a new fitness gadget? Four athletes give their opinion about these gadgets.

Fitness tracker. Daniella, Boston: This is great. You can wear it on your arm or your ankle. It records your steps, your calories, and your sleep. You can use it when you ride a bike, run, walk, play volleyball, do judo, or do any kind of sport. $76. Four and half stars

Underwater headphones. Miguel, Puebla: I love swimming and listening to music at the same time. I can swim really fast when I listen to music. These go around your neck and fit in your ears. They're very comfortable. $200. Three and a half stars.

Sports camera. Felix, Sagres: It can take videos when I'm surfing. But when I'm on my surfboard, I can't hold it in my hand. I put it on my surfboard instead. You can also wear it on your head or on your shoulder. It takes pictures, too. $152. Four stars.

Ankle sensor. Clare, Santa Fe: You wear it on your foot and it checks that you're running correctly. Can you wash it? No, you can't wash it, even when it's dirty. It's expensive, in my opinion, but it's useful for professional runners. $120. Two and a half stars.

Track 02

A: Can you swim?
B: I can.
A: Can you come to a new water polo class with me?
B: Sorry, I can't. I play tennis then.

Track 03

David

This is a ball game we play on the beach. It's a combination of volleyball, soccer, and gymnastics. Oh, and trampolining! And there's music—so young people like to do it. I can throw the ball hard, but I'm not very good at catching it. But my team usually wins!

Claudia

I can't play, but I like watching it. It's like tennis. Three or four players stand in a circle and bounce the ball to the middle. You have to play fast. My friend plays it well, so she usually wins.

Marco

It's an unusual ballgame, but I love it. It helps me stay in shape. It's like golf and soccer. I usually play it in the summer. You have to kick the ball gently. I can kick it easily, but I'm not good at getting the ball into the hole!

Track 04

One of the exercises that I do at the gym is very hard. It's called the deadlift with an overhead press. You stand with your feet on the floor. Then you lift the weight (I use a 10 kilogram) up to your chest. You hold it there for about five seconds. Then you bend your knees and push the weight up above your head. It's not easy to stretch your arms so they're straight. I can usually only hold it above my head for about 10 seconds. I'm amazed how weightlifters do this all the time!

Track 05

Do you work in an office? Do you get tired of sitting all day? Then how about deskercise—exercises you can do at your desk! The first exercise is for your neck. Sit up straight. Bend your neck to your right shoulder. Hold for a few seconds. Then repeat on the left side. The second exercise is good for your shoulders. Stretch your arms slowly above your head and hold for five seconds. Pull your shoulders back. The third exercise is called look around. Turn your head to the left and look over your shoulder. Twist your body and hold for five seconds. Then repeat it on the right side.

The next exercise is for your back. Stand up. Put your hands behind your back. Push your hands together and hold for five to 10 seconds. Pull your shoulders back. And the last exercise—exercise five. Lift one knee up and hold it to your body. Try to hold it for five to 10 seconds. Repeat it with the other leg. These are a few important warm-up deskercises. Try to do these deskercises for five minutes every day.

Track 06

Outdoor Gyms Around the World

Many cities around the world have outdoor gyms. You see them on the beaches of Rio and in the parks in Shanghai or Spain. Here are some different outdoor gyms from around the world.

There is a famous outdoor gym called Muscle Beach in California, USA. Bodybuilders, weightlifters, athletes, and gymnasts train here. It's now a popular tourist attraction and you can buy a ticket to go see the place!

China has many outdoor gyms. This is the outdoor gym in the People's Park in Haikou. About 40% of China's 1.4 billion people use outdoor gyms regularly, according to Top.me. There are about 600,000 outdoor gyms in the country. They are all free!

A new outdoor gym in Sunnymead Park in Oxford, England, has some interesting technology. When people exercise on the machines, they create electricity. The electricity creates power for streetlights, smartphones, or tablets. People who use the outdoor gym can download an app so their doctor can check their health online. Amazing!

Unit 8

Track 01

Wendy, Canada, says …

Hi, food fans! Do you know the word *gastronaut*? It's a person who travels and tries different foods. That's me! I love something delicious called *hagelslag*. It's from the Netherlands. It has small, sweet pieces of chocolate you put on bread for breakfast. My boyfriend thinks it's disgusting! Do you like foods from different countries, too? What kind? How many new dishes do you try each week?

Soraya, Bali, says …

I'm a gastronaut, too! I love to try different foods from all over the world. My favorite food is *tom yum soup*, from Thailand. It's a spicy soup with shrimp and vegetables. I often have it for lunch. It's a very healthy meal! I add chilies to mine to make it extra spicy.

Peter, South Africa, says …

Hi, Wendy! Do you know about *bunny chow*? It comes from South Africa. It's a loaf of bread, but you take the middle of the bread out and put spicy beef or chicken inside. How much meat do you need? It depends on how big the loaf is! We usually eat it for lunch or dinner.

Marlena, Venezuela, says …

My favorite food is *empanadas*. They are delicious. You can make them with corn flour, water, and salt. You can put cheese, meat, chicken—anything you like—inside. Then you fry them. Some people eat them as a snack. My mom thinks they are unhealthy because you fry them.

Ben, Scotland, says …

I think I'm a gastronaut, too. Do you know a dessert called *cendol* from Malaysia? It's really unusual. It's green rice noodles, coconut milk, and sugar. You can also add fruit. It's very sweet. It looks like green spaghetti!

Track 02

Conversation 1

Interviewer: Here we are at the Central Food Market. It's a Saturday morning and it's very busy now. Food markets like this sell cheap food, but is it healthy? Let's ask that woman selling food. This smells delicious! What are you making?

Woman: I'm making falafel. They're, a Middle Eastern snack food. Do you want to try one?

Interviewer: Yes, please!

Woman: OK, here you go. So, this is the falafel. There is salad here, and this is pita bread.

Interviewer: Oh, yum! It's delicious—spicy, too! What's in falafel?

Woman: They are balls made of chickpea flour.

Interviewer: Are they healthy?

Woman: This falafel is healthy because we grill it. Fried falafel has more fat and calories. Falafel is also vegan. There's no meat or dairy in it.

Interviewer: It's They are really delicious! Thank you.

Woman: No problem.

Conversation 2

Interviewer: OK, now let's ask this man what he's eating. Excuse me, what are you eating?

Man: Oh, this is bibimbap. It's Korean. It's a very healthy meal!

Interviewer: What's in it?

Man: Well, this one is a vegetarian dish. Um … there's an egg on top, and there are vegetables and rice. It's delicious!

Interviewer: So, the egg is protein, the rice is a carbohydrate, and there are vegetables—carrots, spinach, and mushrooms. It looks like a balanced meal!

Man: Yes, and it's only $5!

Interviewer: So, the food at this market is delicious, and some of it is healthy, too.

Track 03

Conversation 1

A: Is this my salad? **B:** No, that's your salad.

Conversation 2

A: Are these your apples? **B:** No, those are my apples.

Conversation 3

A: Do you want that snack? **B:** No, I want this one.

Track 04

So, first, the ingredients you need are two cups of flour, one cup of water, and oil. You also need vegetables. Here, I have one cup of delicious red tomatoes, one orange pepper, one green pepper, one cup of corn, and one purple onion. You also need two cups of yellow cheese.

Track 05

To make the pizza dough, put the flour in a bowl. Add salt and pepper. Then add the water and oil. Mix with a spoon or fork. Then use your hands to make a ball. Roll the ball into a circle. Put the pizza dough on a baking dish. Next, slice all the vegetables into small pieces. Don't mix them together. Put the cheese on the pizza dough first. Make a row of tomatoes, then orange peppers, then corn. Next, add green peppers. Then add purple onions. Bake at 200°C for 20 minutes. Then slice. Eat this pizza for lunch. It's also great for a party!

Track 06

Eating Out in Paradissos

Many people like to eat out in a neighborhood called Paradissos. There are a lot of bars and restaurants, and food from around the world, like Thai, Japanese, Greek, French—you name it! Some of the restaurants are great for snacks, but there are some expensive restaurants, too. It's hard to know what's good and what's not, so here is our guide to the places we like in Paradissos …

Matilda's: Vegetarian restaurant. Great for lunch. Healthy food.
We like: the mushroom burger and the delicious avocado salad
We don't like: the carrot cake, there are only five tables
$20 for lunch
Three stars

Yu Garden: Chinese restaurant. Open evenings only.
We like: the chicken noodles and egg fried rice
We don't like: the noise, the open kitchen
$30 for 3 dishes
Four stars

Fred's Fish: Fish and seafood restaurant. Lunch and dinner. Outdoor tables in the summer.
We like: spicy shrimp spaghetti with tomatoes
We don't like: the vegetable dishes, small portions
$40–$60
Three and a half stars

Encore: French café and restaurant. Breakfast, lunch, and dinner.
We like: the steak and fries—so tasty!
We don't like: Nothing—we love everything here!
$25 in the café, $70 in the restaurant
Five stars

Unit 9

Track 01

There but Not There: Virtual Travel

Would you like to visit another continent—Europe, maybe? See Italy or Greece? Or how about a country in Africa, like Kenya? If you want to save time and money when you travel, here's a tip. You need to try virtual tourism! But what is virtual tourism? And how does it work?

When you plan to visit a new place, go online and take a virtual tour first. You can use a virtual reality headset and a computer to take a tour. You don't have to use a computer if you have an app on your smartphone. A virtual tour gives you all the sights and sounds of a place. Take a tour of a street market in a city like Delhi or enjoy tourist attractions in Rio de Janeiro. You can decide what you like to do before you go.

Many people enjoy traveling more when they plan with virtual tours. They like spending time on things that interest them. With virtual tours, they can spend more time on the things they love when they finally get to their dream vacation destination!

Track 02

I want to visit Europe.
Do you like to travel?
I don't have to work on Monday.

Track 03

Host: Today, we're on the streets of cities around the world. We're asking people if they like high season or low season in their city. Excuse me. *Radio English Today*. Can I ask your name?

Manuel: Hello. Yes, it's Manuel.
Host: Think about tourism in your city. Do you like the high season or low season?
Manuel: Well, I live in Barcelona, Spain. We get a lot of tourists every year during the summer. Tourists are good for the economy, but it can be very busy and noisy. I like the winter, when it's quiet. You can always get a table at a restaurant!
Host: Thank you. Hello. What is your name?
Andra: Andra.
Host: Where are you from?
Andra: I'm from Reykjavik, the capital of Iceland.
Host: Do you like high season or low season in Reykjavik?
Andra: It's very dark in the middle of winter and we don't get many tourists then. My favorite time of year is the middle of summer. We have lots of visitors and all the cafés and restaurants are open. There's a lot to do.
Host: Thank you. Here's one more person. Can I ask your name?
Viktor: I'm Viktor.
Host: Viktor, do you like the high season or low season in your city?
Viktor: In Lima, Peru, we get tourists all year, but the high season is October to March. That's in the summer. I like it then because you meet lots of new people from other countries. It's my favorite time of year.
Host: Thank you, Viktor.

Track 04

José
I travel a lot! I like to go to cold countries, like Canada. I usually go for work. When I go there, I take a jacket and gloves. You have to stay warm!
Isabela
When I go on vacation, I like to go to the beach. I like swimming and I always pack a swimsuit. When you go to the beach, you should take something warm for the evening. I take a sweater.
Mike
I should travel more! I like to go to the mountains. I pack boots because I like to hike. I don't take swimsuits or shorts, but I always take lots of socks! You change your socks a lot when you're in the mountains!
Amal
You should look good on vacation! I like to go to interesting cities. When I go on a trip, I take nice blouses. I wear them when I go out to restaurants. I also pack jeans, of course. Those are the clothes I usually take.

Track 05

Detourism
Love or hate it, Venice is a very popular tourist destination. Some people say it's too popular! Around 30 million people visit Venice, Italy, every year. The problem is, they all want to see the same things: the canals, St. Mark's Square, the Doge's Palace. The small city of Venice (population 50,000) attracts large crowds of visitors every year. Tourism is important for the economy of the city, but it's very expensive to keep Venice in good condition.

To deal with this problem, some people suggest detourism. A detour is a short trip in a different direction. Detourism shows tourists attractions that most people don't visit. That way, tourists aren't always in the same place at the same time. For example, when you move away from the canals, Venice also has interesting markets, restaurants, and shops. And there are unusual attractions, such as the multicolored houses on the island of Burano and the Lazzaretto Nuovo, home to the Vampire of Venice! It's a very different side of Venice.

Detourism can lead to many different kinds of vacations and new experiences. Have fun!

Unit 10

Track 01

An Inspiration for All
Malala Yousafzai was born in 1997 in the Swat Valley in Pakistan. Her father was an educator, and he wanted his daughter to get an education. But in 2007 and 2008, the schools for girls closed in her region of Pakistan, and Malala stopped going to school.

Malala wrote a blog for British TV about her life that year. She wanted all girls to have the opportunity to get an education. She became well known in Pakistan. Then in 2011, Malala's school finally opened again. Malala's blog made some powerful people angry. On October 9, 2012, Malala was shot on her way to school. She was only 14 years old.

Malala was lucky. She survived, and her family took her to England. When she was better, she started school there. She continued to talk about education for girls in Pakistan, and she went around the world to speak. In 2013, she started the Malala Fund. In 2014, she won the Nobel Peace Prize. The next year, a film of her life, called *He Named Me Malala*, told her story. In spring 2017, she went around the world on her Girl Power Trip and met world leaders. She asked them to support education for all girls. In autumn 2017, she started to study at Oxford University.

Malala continues to inspire young people around the world.

Track 02

learned stopped decided

Track 03

Luciana: Hi, Madison! How are things in Los Angeles?
Madison: Great! But I'm really tired!
Luciana: Why?
Madison: Well, I met up with friends last night because I didn't have any homework.
Luciana: Where did you go?
Madison: We went out to eat because we were hungry. After that, we saw a movie. I went to bed after 1:00 a.m. because the movie finished late! What did you do last night?
Luciana: Oh, I didn't go out because I had to study. I ordered food online.
Madison: What did you get?
Luciana: I ordered a pizza because the restaurant is close to my house. Then I studied for a few hours until I felt tired and went to bed. That's my boring life! Oh, but I had a great time last weekend!
Madison: Really? What did you do?
Luciana: I went on a date!
Madison: Really? Tell me all about it!
Luciana: Well, it was someone from my English class …

Track 04

Kristina
This happened last year. I went to my cousin's party with some friends. I thought it was just a regular party, but it was her birthday, and I forgot! I didn't take a present or a card or anything. I felt bad, but I got her something the next day.

Javier
I met Isaac a year ago. He joined or soccer team, and he got lost on the way to practice. When I saw him, I showed him where to go. After practice, we went out to eat together. That's how we became good friends.
Lauren
I think this was about two months ago. I made a reservation at a restaurant for me and my friends. But when we got there, they said they didn't have a table for us. We waited for an hour! My friend said I forgot to reserve it, but I did reserve it! It was the restaurant's mistake. We argued, and I got a little upset, to be honest.

Track 05

The World Advice Corner
The world's problem-solving web page
Got a problem? Got a solution? Here at the World Advice Corner, we want you to use your experience to help each other. Post your problem and then read the advice from people around the world. Or find a problem and give your advice. Here's a selection of problems on the World Advice Corner.

My problem is that I'm lonely. It's hard to make new friends. I went to a party recently and spent most of the night in the kitchen! I get nervous around people I don't know. Does anyone have any advice? —Adrian

My parents try to control my life! When I go out with friends, they always want to know exactly where I am and what I'm doing. I have to text them every half an hour or they worry. How can I find a solution? I don't want to argue with them. —Maria

I have a work problem. Last week, I made a mistake and my boss yelled at me. I got upset and didn't know what to do. Did this ever happen to you? What did you do? All advice welcome! —Olivia

Unit 11

Track 01

What to Do about To-Do Lists
What are you going to do today? Maybe you're going to write an important email or take your car to the carwash. Or maybe you are going to shop for a gift, plan an evening with friends, or make a dentist appointment. We all have busy lives and it's easy to forget things we're supposed to do.

A list of things to do—or a "to-do list"—helps us remember what to do, but many people make a big mistake when they write their lists: they list a lot of things and then only do half of them. Here are some tips for writing a useful to-do list.

1 Write three things you are going to do in one day. Choose the things that are really important and write your list the night before. That way, you're ready to go in the morning!

2 When you have more than three things to do, write the top three and do them first. Then, make a new list and write another three things. If you have one big job to do, break it into smaller jobs.

3 Write exactly what you need to do. Don't write "learn English." Write "learn eight new English words." People do things on their lists when it's clear what to do.

4 Be ready to change your list. Things are going to happen that you didn't plan. When they do, write a new list. Life is full of surprises!

Track 02

1 A: What are you going to do this weekend?
B: Oh, I'm going to see my cousins.
2 A: Do you and your friend have any plans for tonight?
B: Yes! We're going to go dancing.
3 A: What do you think about your exams?
B: I'm really worried. I think I'm going to fail!
4 A: It's a beautiful day!
B: Yeah … but it's going to get cold later.

Track 03

Host: Welcome to *Money Talks*, the show about you and your money. Today, we're talking about planning for the future. How can you save money each month? We spoke to two people with different ideas. First, David.
David: I don't earn a lot from my job. I live with my parents, so I don't spend money on rent. I want to save money to rent my own apartment. Last month, I spent a lot of money on food. I bought my lunch. This month, I'm going to make sandwiches for myself. That way, I can save a little money every day.
Host: And this is Patricia.
Patricia: I have a large family, so I'm always giving people birthday gifts! It can be expensive, and I want to save for a vacation. This year, I'm going to make gifts for people. Last week, I made my mom a photo album with pictures of me at different ages. She loved it. Next week, it's my brother's birthday. I'm going to make him a pizza! It's his favorite!

Track 04

Host: Welcome to this week's podcast. Today, we're talking about how to get your dream job. With me is Jade Lewis from the website Careers Now. Jade, how do you get your dream job?
Jade: It isn't easy, but there are some things you can do to make your dreams come true. First, start early. Decide on your dream career now. That gives you time to make a career plan and work on that plan right away.
Host: So the first point is: start early. What else?
Jade: Second, get information. Learn what you can about your dream job. What skills do you need? What courses do you need to take? Information helps you plan.
Host: Great. So the second point is: get information. Anything else?
Jade: Finally, don't give up. It takes hard work to get that dream job, and it doesn't happen immediately. You need to be patient. Maybe you need to do another job first. But with a little luck, you might get there one day.
Host: So, don't give up. Jade, thank you very much for talking to us today. And good luck to all of you. I hope you get your dream job one day!

Track 05

Follow Your Passion
Many of us have a hobby or a free-time activity we love. But is it possible to make that hobby a career? For some people, the answer is "yes." Love baking? Start a cake-making business. Exercise every day? Start a career as a personal trainer. Today, lots of people are finding that social media can help them turn their passion into a career.

Fiorella Pia has an interesting hobby. She takes photographs of food and shares them on a social networking website.

She has a talent for making the food look nice. She has a lot of followers and her pictures are very popular. Now she wants to turn her hobby into a career. She wants to earn money from her photography. She's going to plan carefully. She needs to decide exactly what kind of business to start. She also needs to write a business plan. She's asking all her friends for their advice as she puts together her career plan.

Unit 12

Track 01

The Galapagos Islands

The Galapagos Islands are an amazing place for a tour. There are beautiful sandy beaches, awesome animals, and the people are friendly. Every year, new people learn what the Galapagos Islands have to offer. People can swim, dive, and see nature—the Galapagos has it all!

The islands are near the equator. They don't have seasons like some other places do, but there is a cool season from June to November. The water is colder at that time, and there's less rain, so it's drier. It's a great time for diving around the islands. It's also a good time to see whales, sea lions, and penguins. The temperature is around 21–27°C, and the water is around 18–24°C.

From December to May, the temperature is higher. It's called the warm season. It's more tropical during these months, and the skies are cloudier. It's also wetter than the rest of the year. The ocean is warmer and it's better for swimming. It's also a good time to see iguanas, flamingos, and other tropical birds. The temperature is around 27–32°C. The water is cooler than that, at around 21–26°C.

To get there, you need to go to Ecuador. From Ecuador, you can fly to Baltra Island or San Cristóbal Island, or go by boat. Of course, it's quicker to fly than go by boat. Flights are also cheaper, but then you have to pay for a hotel. A luxury cruise ship is more expensive than a trip on a small boat.

Track 02

Host: And now on *My Travels*, we're talking about waterfalls. My guest is Kerry Davis. Kerry, why do you love waterfalls?

Kerry: I love waterfalls because I'm studying geology at college and waterfalls are great places to learn. Last year, I went to the Iguazu Falls in Argentina and Brazil.

Host: They're beautiful!

Kerry: Yes, they are. The Iguazu River goes through Brazil. When it gets to the border with Argentina, it falls 82 meters. The Iguazu Falls are really interesting. There are many islands in the river, and they create about 300 different waterfalls!

Host: When is a good time to visit?

Kerry: There are fewer tourists at Iguazu between July and October, so that's a good time to visit.

Host: Do you plan to visit other waterfalls?

Kerry: This year, I'm going to visit Niagara Falls, on the border between Canada and the United States. Niagara Falls is 50 meters tall. It's really three waterfalls. A good time to visit is a little earlier than Iguazu, usually June to August. I'm going to go in July.

Host: And after that?

Kerry: Next year, I'm going to visit the Angel Falls in Venezuela. Angel Falls is just one waterfall, and it looks amazing. It's higher than the others, of course. It falls 979 meters. I'm going to visit Angel Falls next May because the water is higher then. It's going to be great!

Host: I hope you can come back and tell us all about your trips. Thank you, Kerry.

Track 03

beautiful	document
communicate	music
cute	popular

Track 04

Tourist: Hello. I'm going to visit Mexico this summer. I want to see an unusual natural place. Do you have any suggestions?

Travel Agent: Yes, of course. Mexico has many amazing natural places. One of them is the volcano called Paricutin. It appeared in a corn field in the state of Michoacán in 1943.

Tourist: What? It wasn't there before? It just … appeared?

Travel Agent: Yes! It grew very quickly. It was the first time scientists saw the birth of a volcano. It's popular with people from all over the world. You can get there by flying to Uruapan and then taking a bus to the village of Angahuan.

Tourist: Are there tours of the volcano?

Travel Agent: Local people take visitors to see the volcano on horseback. It's one to two hours from the town to the volcano. Then you can walk to the top of the volcano.

Tourist: Is it a long trip?

Travel Agent: It takes about six or seven hours. I can show you pictures of the area.

Tourist: Great!

Track 05

Local College Asks for Ideas

By Janice Baskin

Meadowville College is a college near our city. There is a large lake and a forest on Meadowville's campus. Right now, not many people use the lake or the forest. Some people go swimming or camping there in the summer.

Recently, the college decided to use this area for its students. Dean Linda Collins says, "We want our students to learn about nature and learn new skills. Many of our students come from big cities and they don't know a lot about nature. They are more familiar with technology than they are with the natural world." The college wants students to be interested in nature. "They need activities to introduce them to outdoor life. Maybe something that uses technology can get them interested—something that connects nature to their studies," says Dean Collins.

The college is asking students for ideas and suggestions. They have money for the project and they are happy to spend it on the right ideas.

Macmillan Education
4 Crinan Street
London N1 9XW
A division of Macmillan Education Limited

Companies and representatives throughout the world

Speak Your Mind Level 1B Student's Book
ISBN 978-138-003-110-5
Speak Your Mind Level 1B Student's Book + access to Student's App and Digital Workbook ISBN 978-138-003-856-2
Speak Your Mind Level 1B Student's Book + access to Student's App
ISBN 978-138-003-857-9

Text, design, and illustration © Macmillan Education Limited 2020
Written by Mickey Rogers, Joanne Taylore-Knowles, and Steve Taylore-Knowles

The authors have asserted their right to be identified as the authors of this work in accordance with the Copyright, Designs, and Patents Act 1988.

First published 2020

All rights reserved. No part of this publication may be reproduced, stored in a retrieval system, or transmitted in any form or by any means, electronic, mechanical, photocopying, recording, or otherwise, without the prior written permission of the publishers.

Designed by QBS Learning
Illustrated by Jerome Brasseur (Beehive Illustration) pp. 68(t), 110; Daniel Deamo (Lemonade Illustration) pp. 81, 90, 153; Keith Favazza (Wendy Lynn & Co.) pp. 70, 75; Bunky Hurter (Mendola Artists) pp. 82, 92; QBS Learning pp. 68(c), 80.
Original cover design by therestless.co.uk
Cover adaptation by Roberto Martinez
Cover photographs by **Getty Images**/PeopleImages (upper body), Getty Images/Tim Robberts (lower body), Getty Images/Chatuporn Sornlampoo/EyeEm (background); **Shutterstock**/REDPIXEL.PL (window).

Picture research by Fernanda Rocha/Ikonia LLC

Authors' acknowledgements
Mickey, Jo and Steve would like to thank everyone at Macmillan Education and RedNova Learning who have made this project possible and who have gone the extra mile (literally!) to meet up, work together, and throw around a million ideas, some of which even made their way into the books! Jo and Steve would also like to thank Scout for her patience and understanding and for letting her parents get on with it when they needed to!

The publishers would like to thank all the teachers that piloted and reviewed the series, and a special thanks to Annette Flavel for content and cultural reviews.

The authors and publishers would like to thank the following for permission to reproduce their photographs:
Alamy Stock Photo/Alamy Stock Photo/Buiten-Beeld p. 118(mr), Alamy Stock Photo/Cliff Hide General News p. 74(r), Alamy Stock Photo/Lev Dolgachov p. 72(1), Alamy Stock Photo/Vadym Drobot p. 101(r), Alamy Stock Photo/Thanapol Kuptanisakorn p. 100(b), Alamy Stock Photo/Robert Preston Photography p. 122(tl), Alamy Stock Photo/Dmitry Rukhlenko – Travel Photos p. 72(8); **Getty Images**/Afonskaya p. 124, Getty Images/AFP/TONY KARUMBA p. 98(br), Getty Images/Robert Alexander p. 120(bl), Getty Images/ullstein bild p. 122(tcr), Getty Images/Blend Images/Mike Kemp p. 72(3), Getty Images/bowdenimages p. 112(3), Getty Images/Paul_Brighton p. 78(cl), Getty Images/CaiaImage/Dan Dalton, Getty Images/Cosmo Condina p. 120(tl), Getty Images/Peter Dazeley p. 82(2), Getty Images/Reza Estakhrian p. 112(1), Getty Images/E+/AJ_Watt p. 101(l), Getty Images/E+/filadendron p. 105(6), Getty Images/E+/franckreporter p. 105(7), Getty Images/E+/GCShutter p. 101(b), Getty Images/E+/Neustockimages p. 114(bl), Getty Images/E+/olaser p. 105(5), Getty Images/E+/shapecharge p. 112(5), Getty Images/E+/xavierarnau p. 93(4), Getty Images/E+/Gang Zhou p. 72(4), Getty Images/E+/jcrosemann p. 107(wallpaper), Getty Images/Michele Falzone p. 122(tcl), Getty Images/Pawel Gaul p. 122(br), Getty Images/Ghislain & Marie David de Lossy p. 114(br), Getty Images/gregobagel p. 74(l), Getty Images/Tom Grill p. 102(1), Getty Images/Craig Hastings pp. 120(ml), 122(bc), Getty Images/Image Source p. 112(6), Getty Images/iStock/jeremyiswild p. 102(2), Getty Images/iStock/masta4650 p. 72(2), Getty Images/iStock/Netalieh p. 82(9), Getty Images/iStock/padchas p. 119, Getty Images/iStock/RapidEye p. 108, Getty Images/Jacobs Stock Photography Ltd p. 112(4), Getty Images/Juice Images/altrendo images p. 117, Getty Images/Lonely Planet Images/Michael Marquand p. 120(br), Getty Images/Jiu Mei Zuo M/EyeEm p. 120(tr), Getty Images/Morsa Images p. 72(7), Getty Images/MuYeeTing p. 122(bl), Getty Images/National Geographic Image Collection Magazines/Jonathan Kingston p. 74(m), Getty Images/Jose Luis Pelaez Inc. p. 100(t), Getty Images/Edwin Remsberg p. 120(bcl), Getty Images/Selitbul p. 120(tcr), Getty Images/Steve Smith p. 121, Getty Images/Lisa Stirling p. 82(8), Getty Images/Richard Stonehouse/Stringer p. 98(tr), Getty Images/Tetra Images p. 113, Getty Images/tororo p. 123, Getty Images/MARIO VAZQUEZ/Stringer p. 122(tr), Getty Images/Klaus Vedfelt p. 112(2), Getty Images/Andreas Vitting p. 120(tcl), Getty Images/Vostok p. 84, Getty Images/Michele Westmorland p. 118(tl); **Macmillan Publishers**/David Tolley p. 82(5); **Shutterstock**/Africa Studio pp. 82(4), 107(man), Shutterstock/Wan Faidz p. 78(cr), Shutterstock/fizkes p. 102(3), Shutterstock/baranq p. 72(cr), Shutterstock/Orhan Cam pp. 126, 138, Shutterstock/George Dolgikh p. 85, Shutterstock/GK1982 p. 107(boy), Shutterstock/KucherAV p. 110, Shutterstock/ESB Professional pp. 6, Shutterstock/Yuriy Golub p. 72(5), Shutterstock/Barbara Maffei Granadillo p. 78(c), Shutterstock/haveseen p. 93(2), Shutterstock/Jirsak p. 135, Shutterstock/Jyliana p. 77, Shutterstock/Lighthunter p. 97, Shutterstock/Jacob Lund p. 87, Shutterstock/mates p. 82(10), Shutterstock/Jaroslav Moravcik p. 94, Shutterstock/Tony Northrup p. 120(bcr), Shutterstock/Pressmaster pp. 86, 136, Shutterstock/Prostock-studio p. 102(4), Shutterstock/repbone p. 137, Shutterstock/George Rudy p. 67, Shutterstock/Shooting Star Studio p. 99, Shutterstock/Tong_stocker p. 93(1), Shutterstock/Syda Productions p. 88, Shutterstock/Awirut Somsanguan p. 78(r), Shutterstock/Suriya99 p. 93(tl), Shutterstock/Sergey Tinyakov p. 93(3), Shutterstock/Denis Val p. 114(mr), Shutterstock/WAYHOME studio p. 104; **Superstock**/Matt Dutile/Image Source p. 54; **123RF**/ammentorp p. 72(6).

Additional Sources:
p. 106, *Planet Wedding: A Nuptial-pedia*, by Sandra Choron and Harry Choron, 2010, Mariner Books. p. 106, "Fun Facts About Birthdays," 2017, PaperStyle website. p. 106, "12 Fun Facts About Wedding Planning," by Stefania Sainato, 2012, *Bridal Guide Magazine*. p. 126, "Want Real Job Satisfaction? Be a Gardener or a Florist: 90% of Horticulturalists Enjoy Going to Work," by Paul Sims, November 12, 2012, *Daily Mail* website. p. 126, "11 Scientific Benefits of Being Outdoors," 2019, *Mental Floss* website.

These materials may contain links for third party websites. We have no control over, and are not responsible for, the contents of such third party websites. Please use care when accessing them.

The inclusion of any specific companies, commercial products, trade names or otherwise does not constitute or imply its endorsement or recommendation by Macmillan Education Limited.

Printed and bound in Mexico
by Compañía Editorial Ultra, S.A. de C.V.

2021 2020
13 12 11 10